# OLIVER GOLDSMITH
## AND
# RICHARD BRINSLEY SHERIDAN

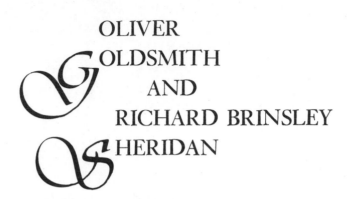

# OLIVER GOLDSMITH AND RICHARD BRINSLEY SHERIDAN

MARLIES K. DANZIGER

WITH HALFTONE ILLUSTRATIONS

FREDERICK UNGAR PUBLISHING CO.

NEW YORK

*Copyright © 1978 by Frederick Ungar Publishing Co., Inc.*
*Printed in the United States of America*
*Designed by Edith Fowler*

*Library of Congress Cataloging in Publication Data*

*Danziger, Marlies K*
  *Oliver Goldsmith and Richard Brinsley Sheridan.*

  *(World dramatists series)*
  *Bibliography: p.*
  *Includes index.*
  *1.  Goldsmith, Oliver, 1728-1774—Comedies.  2. Sheridan, Richard Brinsley Butler, 1751-1816—Criticism and interpretation.*
  *PR3494.D3      822'.6'08      77-6946*
  *ISBN 0-8044-2129-3*

# CONTENTS

# CHRONOLOGY

---

* Many dates in Goldsmith's life are uncertain because of his own reticence, the lack of public records, and the absence of a full biography in his lifetime. This chronology is based largely on A. Lytton Sells, Oliver Goldsmith: His Life and Works (London and New York, 1974), pp. 21-190, passim.

1759        Published translation, *Memoirs of the Life
            of M. de Voltaire; Enquiry into the Present
            State of Polite Learning in Europe*; and *The
            Bee*.

1760–61     *Chinese Letters* appeared serially in *Public
            Ledger*.

1762        *Chinese Letters* published as *The Citizen of
            the World*.
            October 28: Rescued from arrest for debt
            by Dr. Samuel Johnson, who used manu-
            script of *The Vicar of Wakefield* to raise
            money.

1764        Published *A History of England*.
            Became member of Dr. Johnson's newly
            founded Literary Club.
            December 19: *The Traveller: A Prospect of
            Society* published.

1766        *The Vicar of Wakefield* published.

1767        Wrote *The Good-Natured Man*.

1768        *The Good-Natured Man* opened at Covent
            Garden.

1769        *Roman History*, reworking of lengthy his-
            tory in French, published. Acquired honor-
            ary title of Professor of Ancient History in
            the Royal Academy.

1770        May 26: *The Deserted Village* published
            and became an immediate success.
            July: Visited France in company of friends.

1771        Began *Mistakes of a Night*, later called *She
            Stoops to Conquer*.

1773        January 1: "An Essay on the Theatre; or,
            A Comparison Between Laughing and Sen-
            timental Comedy" published in *Westminster
            Magazine*.
            March 15: *She Stoops to Conquer* opened
            at Covent Garden.
            May 8: *The Grumbler*, a one-act farce,
            performed for one night at Covent Garden.
            Worked on *Grecian History*.

1774      Finished *An History of the Earth and Animated Nature.*
April 4: Died after short illness.

## RICHARD BRINSLEY SHERIDAN\*

1751      September or October: Born in Dublin.

1762–67, 68 or 69      Student at Harrow.

1766      Mother died in France.

1770–72      Moved to Bath with father and siblings. Met Elizabeth Linley.

1772      March: Accompanied Elizabeth Linley to France to help her escape advances of Captain Thomas Mathews.
May 4: On return to England, duel in London with Captain Mathews.
July 1: Second duel with Captain Mathews on Kingsdown near Bath.

1773      April 13: Married Elizabeth Linley.

1774      Wrote *The Rivals*.

1775      January 17: *The Rivals* opened at Covent Garden.
May 2: *St. Patrick's Day* opened at Covent Garden.
November 17: Son Thomas born.
November 21: Became manager of Drury Lane theater, taking over from David Garrick.

1777      February 24: *A Trip to Scarborough*, adapted from Sir John Vanbrugh's *The Relapse*, opened at Drury Lane.
March: Became member of Dr. Samuel Johnson's Literary Club.

---

\* *This chronology is based largely on Madeleine Bingham,* Sheridan: The Track of a Comet *(New York, 1972) and* Jack D. Durant, Richard Brinsley Sheridan *(Boston, 1975),* pp. *15-32.*

|      | May 8: *The School for Scandal* opened at Drury Lane. |
|------|-------------------------------------------------------|
| 1779 | March 12: Payed tribute to David Garrick, just deceased, in "Verses to the Memory of Garrick: Spoken as a Monody at the Theatre Royal in Drury Lane."<br>October 29: *The Critic* opened at Drury Lane. |
| 1780 | September 12: Elected Member of Parliament. Continued to manage Drury Lane. |
| 1782 | March–July: Served as Under-Secretary of State for Foreign Affairs. |
| 1783 | February–December: Served as Secretary to the Treasury. |
| 1787 | February 7: Gave celebrated speech in Parliament against Warren Hastings, impeached for corruption in management of East India Company. |
| 1792 | March 30: Daughter Mary born.<br>June 28: Wife Elizabeth died.<br>October: Daughter Mary died.<br>Drury Lane theater, reported unsafe, torn down. |
| 1794 | April 21: Rebuilt and greatly enlarged Drury Lane theater reopened. |
| 1795 | Married Esther (or Hester) Ogle. |
| 1796 | Son Charles Brinsley ("Robin") born. |
| 1799 | May 24: *Pizarro*, adapted from August von Kotzebue's *Die Spanier in Peru*, opened at Drury Lane. |
| 1809 | Fire burned down Drury Lane theater. |
| 1812 | Lost seat in Parliament. |
| 1816 | Died in poverty. |

All quotations from the plays are taken from Arthur Friedman, *Collected Works of Oliver Goldsmith*, 5 vols. (Oxford, 1966) and Cecil Price, *The Dramatic Works of Richard Brinsley Sheridan*, 2 vols. (Oxford, 1973).

# GOLDSMITH, SHERIDAN, AND THEIR WORLD

Oliver Goldsmith and Richard Brinsley Sheridan, writing their plays in the late 1760s and 1770s, are famous for bringing genuine, funny comedy back to the English stage after a lengthy period when "genteel," sentimental comedy was in vogue. David Garrick's Prologue to Goldsmith's *She Stoops to Conquer* (1773) has an actor dressed in mourning declare that "The Comic muse, long sick, is now a dying!" and that Goldsmith is the doctor who has come to her aid. The same may be said of Sheridan. Although sentimental comedy was not quite as lachrymose as is generally believed, and Goldsmith and Sheridan were not alone in criticizing it, they managed, within a span of four years, to produce three outstanding comedies —*She Stoops to Conquer* (1773), *The Rivals* (1775), and *The School for Scandal* (1777)—comedies that indeed are extraordinarily amusing and have remained a part of the English and American repertory to this day.

Although Goldsmith and Sheridan had similar aims —to oppose the sentimental vogue of their time—they differed in their points of view and, to some extent, in their achievements. Goldsmith was essentially conservative, valuing the time-honored standards of the family and society. Sheridan tended to be a gadfly, questioning parental authority and the Establishment. Goldsmith is usually credited with humor; Sheridan, with wit. Goldsmith has been called—although not without some exaggeration—the Shakespeare of eighteenth-century comedy; Sheridan, the Congreve. A study of the major plays of both writers heightens one's awareness of these differences as well as drawing attention to a moment of vitality in English comedy that was not to be repeated for more than a century.

Goldsmith was a mature man when he wrote his two plays. Indeed, he produced them toward the end of a varied, at times aimless, and often not particularly happy life. He was born in Ireland and became one of those displaced Irishmen—Sheridan was another—who made their reputations in England.

The year of Goldsmith's birth—1728 or 1730—is uncertain, as are other facts about his life. It is known, however, that his father was an impoverished clergyman and that young Oliver went to several local schools. An amusing anecdote recorded by Goldsmith's sister remains from these early years. Traveling home from school in Edgeworthstown, Oliver supposedly mistook a local squire's house for an inn and spent the night there under this misapprehension. Although it is doubtful that he could really have remained mistaken for so long,[1] he reworked this episode brilliantly in *She Stoops to Conquer.*

Goldsmith studied at Trinity College, Dublin, passing his final examinations in 1749 or 1750. Then, unsure of what career to choose, he made a number of false starts. At the urging of his family, he tried to become a clergyman but was rejected by the local bishop, who seems to have recognized Goldsmith's lack of vocation. He worked briefly as a private tutor. He attempted to go to America but missed the boat in Cork and returned home. He set out for London to study law but got only as far as Dublin, where he lost his money at cards and again returned home. In 1752 he managed to get to Edinburgh, where he studied law for more than a year.

Early in 1754 Goldsmith went to the Continent. He spent several months in Holland, studying in Leyden, and then traveled through France, Switzerland, and Italy. He was perpetually short of money; legend has it that he paid for his board and lodging by playing his flute or by engaging in debates at monasteries on his way.

Back in England in February 1756, Goldsmith once more cast around for a suitable occupation. For two years he alternated between attempting to teach and to practice medicine. Although he was twice turned down for medical positions, he adopted the title "Doctor" during this time.

In 1757, Goldsmith turned to professional writing. He began with articles, reviews, and translations from the French. Finally, in 1759, he tried his hand at more original writings. His *Enquiry into the Present State of Polite Learning in Europe* (1759), a lengthy essay on the declining state of learning in England and on the Continent, did not create much attention. But then Goldsmith found a more attractive medium in the short essay. *The Bee*, a series of lively essays on a variety of topics, appeared once a week from October 6 to November 24, 1759. It was soon followed by the even livelier and more popular *Chinese Letters*, published serially in 1760–61 and in book form, under the title *The Citizen of the World*, in the following year.

In 1761 Goldsmith made the acquaintance of the much-admired man of letters Dr. Samuel Johnson, who became his friend and protector. It was thanks to Dr. Johnson that *The Vicar of Wakefield*, one of Goldsmith's best-loved works, was published. Apparently Dr. Johnson came to his friend's rescue one day in 1762 when Goldsmith was about to be arrested for debt. Dr. Johnson took the manuscript of the novel to the printer John Newbery and returned with the necessary cash. A few years later Dr. Johnson invited Goldsmith to become a member of his newly founded Literary Club.

During most of the 1760s, Goldsmith made a meager to moderate living from his adaptations, digests, and translations. He compiled extensive histories of England, Rome, and Greece that were to be used for many years in schools. At the same time, he began to make his literary reputation. His first success was the descriptive poem *The Traveller: A Prospect of Society* (1764), based on the observations he had made during his Continental travels. *The Vicar of Wakefield* was finally published in 1766. A seemingly heartwarming narrative about a simple family beset by misfortunes, but actually an ironic survey of the family's follies and the occasional blindness of the vicar himself, the novel was soon greatly admired both in England and abroad. *The Good-Natured Man* (1768), Goldsmith's first play, was less well received, but the long descriptive poem *The Deserted Village* (1770), nostalgically recalling the idyllic village of "sweet Auburn," was a great success. In 1771 he began his second comedy, initially called *Mistakes of a Night*, but eventually retitled *She Stoops to Conquer*, which was staged in March 1773 and brought him new fame. A few months before the opening night, Goldsmith published "An Essay on the Theatre; or, A Comparison Between Laughing and Sentimental Comedy" (1773), criticizing the comedies popular in his day and explaining the kind of comedy that he wished to see revived.

Although *She Stoops to Conquer* proved to be Goldsmith's last important work, he continued to write. He adapted a one-act farce, *The Grumbler* (1773), from Sir Charles Sedley's translation of a French play. The farce was staged only once for the benefit of the actor John Quick, who had played Tony Lumpkin so well in *She Stoops to Conquer*. In addition, Goldsmith completed a huge compendium of zoological lore, *An History of the Earth and Animated Nature*, published after his death. In March 1774, Goldsmith became seriously ill and died a few days later. He was buried in the Temple Burying Ground and is commemorated in Westminster Abbey by a medallion portrait with a Latin epigram by Dr. Johnson.

For much of his life, Goldsmith was a lonely man, professionally and socially insecure, easily insulted, envious of others, and often unhappy. Only in his last years did he find a circle of congenial friends. He may have had a romantic attachment to a young lady called Mary Horneck, and in the summer of 1770 he revisited France in the company of Mary, her mother, and her sister. Although his financial position also improved, he seems to have been irresponsible about money throughout his life, and he was soft-hearted to a fault. Stories abound about his giving away his last penny to some unknown person with a hard-luck story. All the more remarkable, then, are his two stage comedies: *The Good-Natured Man*, with its sharp ridicule of the excessively good-hearted type, and *She Stoops to Conquer*, with its cheerful, good-humored, and humane depiction of romantic and family experiences that were, for the most part, lacking in Goldsmith's own life.

Whereas Goldsmith wrote his plays in mellow maturity, Sheridan wrote his comedies in his twenties, in the full exuberance of youth. Moreover, whereas Goldsmith only slowly made a place for himself in the literary circles of London, Sheridan was part of the theater world from his earliest years.

An Irishman like Goldsmith, Sheridan was born in Dublin in September or October 1751. His father Thomas Sheridan was an actor and, for a time, the manager of a Dublin theater. Sheridan's mother Frances was a minor writer, who produced short novels and a play that may have influenced her son. Richard went to school at Harrow and remained there when his family moved to France. His mother died abroad.

In 1770 Richard joined his father and siblings in the resort town of Bath. Together with a friend, he wrote his first play, *Ixion* (1770), a burlesque in the form of a play rehearsal that was never staged but prefigured *The Critic* (1779). He also met the sixteen-year-old Elizabeth Linley, an attractive singer who was the daughter of the musician Thomas Linley. Through her he became involved in a complicated romantic intrigue. Elizabeth had been pursued first by a rich older man and then by the married Captain Thomas Mathews. To help her escape Mathews's advances and probably already in love with her, Sheridan accompanied

Elizabeth to France. When they returned to England two months later, he was drawn into a duel with Mathews, who had published insulting statements in the Bath *Chronicle*. This duel, an absurd fiasco that left Mathews beaten and forced to apologize, was followed by a second duel, provoked by Mathews, that left Sheridan defeated and wounded.[2] A year later, notwithstanding the disapproval of both Thomas Sheridan and Thomas Linley, Richard married Elizabeth, and the couple settled in London. Their son Thomas was born in 1775.

Sheridan's early London years were extraordinarily productive. Reworking his recent experiences with rivals, duels, and disapproving fathers, he wrote *The Rivals*, which opened at Covent Garden in January 1775. This was followed in May by *St. Patrick's Day; or, The Scheming Lieutenant*, a farce written for the benefit of the actor Lawrence Clinch, who had helped make *The Rivals* a success. In November 1775, the comic opera *The Duenna*, for which his father-in-law and brother-in-law provided the music, was staged at Covent Garden and immediately became a huge success.

But Sheridan had ambitions that went beyond playwriting. In 1776 he took the opportunity to buy a share of the Drury Lane theater, whose manager, the great actor-director David Garrick, wished to retire. For many years Sheridan faced—or tried to evade—the artistic and financial problems involved in keeping this respected London theater afloat.

Sheridan's first work for his new theater was an adaptation of Sir John Vanbrugh's *The Relapse* (1697), produced under the title *A Trip to Scarborough* (1777). Sheridan retained Vanbrugh's hilarious situations and most of the original dialogue but eliminated the risqué passages. Working with Vanbrugh's witty lines undoubtedly influenced him in his next and most brilliant social comedy, *The School for Scandal*, which opened at Drury Lane in May 1777. Two years later he produced one more important comedy, *The Critic* (1779), a lively satire of the theater world and a burlesque of the high-flown heroic drama popular throughout the eighteenth century. Thereafter he collaborated on a number of plays, including the musical entertainment *The Camp* (1778) and *Robinson Crusoe; or, Harlequin Friday* (1781), a sketchy pantomime based partly on Daniel Defoe's *Robinson Crusoe* and partly on the *commedia dell' arte*. But he created no further comedies of his own.

In 1780, Sheridan took up yet another career by going into politics. He was elected Member of Parliament, became friendly with the Whig party leader Charles James Fox, and briefly held the offices of Under-Secretary of State for Foreign Affairs and Secretary of the Treasury. Putting his theatrical talents to new use, he made a name for himself as a brilliant public speaker. The climax of his political career came in 1787 with his five-hour speech in Parliament denouncing Warren Hastings, the former commissioner of India, who was impeached for corruption in the management of the East India Company. It is now far from clear that Hastings deserved Sheridan's harsh criticism or that Sheridan knew enough about the case to justify his position,[3] but there is no doubt that Sheridan turned Parliament and public opinion against Hastings.

This high point was followed by several changes in Sheridan's fortunes. In 1792, Elizabeth died a few months after giving birth to a daughter, and the infant died shortly thereafter. In the same year, the Drury Lane theater, which had been reported unsafe, was torn down. Two years later, the reconstructed Drury Lane, greatly enlarged, reopened. It was there that Sheridan enjoyed one more literary triumph, *Pizarro* (1799), a sentimental tragedy quite unlike his earlier plays, adapted from August von Kotzebue's *Die Spanier in Peru* (1795). Meanwhile, his personal life had improved, for in 1795 he married the twenty-two-year-old Esther (or Hester) Ogle, daughter of the Dean of Winchester. Their son was born in 1796.

The end of Sheridan's life proved to be full of disappointments. In 1809 fire destroyed the new Drury Lane theater, and the financial problems resulting from that fire plagued Sheridan for the rest of his life. His second marriage was far from happy. He lost his seat in Parliament in 1812 and spent his last years in ill health, living in squalid surroundings. Ironically, he died in poverty in 1816 but was honored with a public funeral and burial in Westminster Abbey.

As a young man, Sheridan must have been very attractive—debonair, talented, and enterprising. But he also had a streak of indolence that made it difficult for him to complete his writing in good time. According to legend, he had to be locked into a room at the theater to finish *The School for Scandal*, and when he wrote the words "finished at last, Thank God! R. B. Sheridan" at the end of the manuscript, the prompter could not resist adding "Amen. W. Hopkins."[4] Once Sheridan tasted success, he seems to have become something of a social climber, not averse to courting society ladies who could help his career. Easily bored, and perhaps also afraid that he could never equal his earlier successes, he gave up writing comedies before he was thirty. Yet it is on his comedies that his literary reputation rests. Dr. Johnson recognized Sheridan's achievement when he invited him to join the Literary Club in 1777, commenting: "He who has written the two best comedies of his age, is surely a considerable man."[5]

Goldsmith and Sheridan wrote at a time when two different literary and philosophical traditions were converging. On the one hand, neoclassicism, dominant in the late seventeenth and early eighteenth century, still exerted an influence with its emphasis on good sense, wit, and moderation, and its satires of knaves and fools who lacked these qualities. Neoclassic writings usually reflected the pessimistic philosophy of Thomas Hobbes, who regarded people as basically selfish and considered society essential to hold them in check. Furthermore, as the very term *neoclassicism* suggests, classical antiquity and literary traditions in general were admired, as were tightly organized works, strong in symmetry and balance, that recalled the great works of ancient Greece and Rome.

On the other hand, sentimentalism, which became increasingly prominent in the mid-eighteenth century, dominated the taste of Goldsmith's and Sheridan's time. It valued feeling—one's own emotional experiences and fellow-feelings for others. It extolled the good heart, the signs of which were charitable deeds and tears of sympathy. And it inspired a literature that was heart-warming—at times even tear-jerking. Sentimental writings usually reflected the optimistic philosophy known as benevolism, the belief that people are basically good and that those who are not good have been corrupted by society, especially the fashionable society of the town. In addition, experiments with looser, more flexible forms became popular.

Goldsmith and Sheridan, endowed with that typically English gift for choosing the middle of the road, managed to combine the best of the two traditions in a number of ways. Most notably, they valued both good sense and a good heart, and they coupled a keen insight into human foolishness with a warmth of feeling for their characters.

Still, both writers regarded themselves primarily as opponents of the excessive sentimentalism they saw around them—a sentimentalism that, they believed, had especially ruined stage comedy, making it hardly recognizable as comedy any more. Although one should not disregard the fact that the best of the so-called sentimental comedies were quite lively and amusing, it is true that they had a goodly number of characters in pitiful circumstances who were rescued by heroes or heroines with strikingly good hearts, and that part of their appeal was to the audience's sympathy or admiration. They also tended to milk their scenes for sentiment, prolonging heart-rending moments of recognition and forgiveness or edifying moments of selflessness. Furthermore, an excessive refinement or gentility, bordering on prudishness, had apparently become fashionable in the 1760s and 1770s. Audiences enjoyed high-minded protestations and extended moralizing but frowned on broadly funny scenes or coarse language, perhaps for fear of disrupting the prevailing tender mood.[6]

Goldsmith had no patience with this kind of drama. In his "Essay on the Theatre; or, A Comparison Between Laughing and Sentimental Comedy" (1773) he declared the "Weeping Sentimental Comedy, so much in fashion at Present," greatly inferior to the "Laughing and even Low Comedy" that had been popular until the early eighteenth century. Recognizing that sentimental comedy aimed at pathos, which is more properly the province of tragedy than of comedy, he described it in memorable terms as "a kind of *mulish* production, with all the defects of its opposite parents, and marked with sterility." Indeed, Goldsmith pointed out that sentimental comedy contradicts the very essence of comedy, which is to make us laugh at follies, foibles, or vices—not to make us admire virtue or sympathize with those in distress. Furthermore, he particularly attacked what he considered the confused moral values in sentimental comedies:

> In these Plays almost all the Characters are good, and exceedingly generous . . . and though they want Humour, have abundance of Sentiment and Feeling. If they happen to have Faults or Foibles, the Spectator is taught not only to pardon, but to applaud them, in consideration of the goodness of their heart; so that Folly, instead of being ridiculed, is commended . . .[7]

In short, Goldsmith complained that the faults of the sentimental hero were often overlooked or condoned merely because he had a good heart. As for Sheridan, he was less of a theorist than Goldsmith, but he, too, had no desire to support "The goddess of the woeful countenance—/The sentimental Muse."[8] And both Goldsmith and Sheridan took every opportunity to ridicule characters who had absurd sentimental tendencies.

Yet Goldsmith and Sheridan were not wholly

opposed to the cult of sentiment, and the extent to which they themselves were sentimental, in a negative sense, while ostensibly attacking the sentimentalism of their contemporaries, has remained a subject of continuing debate among modern critics. In considering this aspect of their work, one should keep in mind that there is a difference between valuing sentiment—the good heart—as an important test of a character's worth and valuing sentiment exclusively, excessively, or unreasonably. There is a second, still greater difference between valuing sentiment in a character and creating dramatic scenes in which the characters' and spectators' sentiments are milked by the prolongation or exaggeration of pathetic moments. In short, we should bear in mind the difference between the cult of sentiment, in which Goldsmith and Sheridan to some extent participated, and the emotional exploitations associated with sentimentality in the negative sense, in which they may or may not have indulged.

As they worked to revive "laughing" comedy, Goldsmith and Sheridan were keenly aware of the many kinds of comedy that had flourished in earlier periods. They did not hesitate to be eclectic, deriving incidents and characters from the Roman playwrights Plautus and Terence, from Shakespeare, Ben Jonson, Molière, and many others. Following the tradition of Shakespeare, Ben Jonson, and the English Restoration playwrights of the late seventeenth century, Goldsmith and Sheridan delighted in intricate plots, with enough misunderstandings, disguises, mistaken identities, pranks, tests of character, and surprise revelations to fill two or three comedies. Furthermore, going directly counter to the prevailing taste of their own time but probably with the model of Shakespeare in mind, they relished inserting scenes of farce and other "low" material in the midst of more sophisticated comedy, and they were not afraid to introduce coarse, earthy language when warranted by the character of the speakers. In addition, they liked putting together type characters from different sources—bullying fathers from Roman comedy, benevolent father-figures from Shakespeare, humorous eccentrics from Ben Jonson, country bumpkins from William Wycherley or Sir John Vanbrugh. Extraordinarily amusing in and of themselves, the comedies of Goldsmith and Sheridan offer additional pleasure to modern audiences if we recognize how ingeniously elements of earlier comedies have been combined into lively new wholes.

Yet the plays of Goldsmith and Sheridan pose two major problems to modern audiences. One is that the enormously intricate plots may strike us as artificial and contrived. Perhaps we can be more sympathetic to such plots if we bear in mind that they are part of a long and honorable tradition going back to Roman comedy and continuing, especially in England, from Shakespeare to the end of the eighteenth century. We should bear in mind, moreover, that these plots were profoundly meaningful in Goldsmith's and Sheridan's time because they reflected the generally accepted view of the world—a view best expressed by Alexander Pope at the beginning of *An Essay on Man* that the universe is "a mighty maze, but not without a plan." The general pattern or movement of the plays— confusion eventually resolved into order, coupled with benevolent father-figures—is really a paradigm for the orderly universe and the benevolent deity that constituted the established cosmology in the eighteenth century. For us, who tend to see the world as muddled and chaotic and who are accustomed to black comedy with its sporadic violence and absurdity, there is a certain nostalgia in watching these more optimistic plays. And we also have the pleasure of seeing the extraordinarily skillful plotting and scheming with which Goldsmith and Sheridan bring their highly wrought, intricate actions to a happy conclusion.

The second problem for modern audiences has to do with Goldsmith's and Sheridan's liking for type characters that may strike us as hackneyed and unoriginal. Again, we should remember that this is part of a comic tradition going as far back as the Roman plays and that it is in keeping with the playwrights' admiration for earlier literature as well as with their interest in creating universally understandable characters. Moreover, although we may be taken aback by the regular appearance of pairs of lovers, overbearing parents or guardians, fools from the town or the country, or comic Irishmen, we can also find pleasure in seeing the playwrights ring unexpected changes on these familiar types. In any case, we should bear in mind that modern comedies, too, tend to dramatize types. Perhaps foibles, follies, or vices are worth ridiculing only if they belong to more than a single individual.

As for the actual theaters, these naturally influenced Goldsmith and Sheridan in their work. Only two houses, the Theatre Royal in Drury Lane and the Theatre Royal in Covent Garden, were licensed to give performances in the official winter season. Both of Goldsmith's comedies and the first three of Sheridan's were staged at Covent Garden; *The School for Scandal* and *The Critic* were staged at Drury Lane after Sheridan became its manager in 1776. A minor playhouse, the Little Theatre in the Haymarket, run by the enterprising actor-manager Samuel Foote, was permitted to give plays in the summer months[9] when the other theaters were closed and repeatedly offered *She Stoops to Conquer.*

Plays were performed in repertory and were therefore given only a limited number of performances each year. An evening at the theater tended to be long; the main play was usually followed by an "afterpiece" —a farce or some other entertainment. The afterpieces themselves could be extensive; Sheridan's *St. Patrick's Day* and *The Critic*, billed as afterpieces, are two and three acts respectively.

Actors and actresses were often typecast, and, inversely, some of the parts appear to have been written expressly for certain actors. Edward Shuter, known for his portrayal of older men, played Mr. Croaker in *The Good-Natured Man*, Mr. Hardcastle in *She Stoops to Conquer*, and Sir Anthony Absolute in *The Rivals*. John Quick, famous in broad comic parts, played not only the country-bumpkin squires Tony Lumpkin in *She Stoops to Conquer* and Bob Acres in *The Rivals* but also the ludicrous Isaac Mendoza in *The Duenna*. Lawrence Clinch, who made a success of Sir Lucius O'Trigger in *The Rivals* after John Lee ruined the part on opening night, was rewarded by having *St. Patrick's Day* written for his benefit and getting the lively role of Lieutenant O'Connor. As in our own day, actors could make or break a play, and problems arose when an actor was miscast or had failed to master his lines.

The stage for which Goldsmith and Sheridan wrote their plays was close to that of our own conventional theaters. A proscenium arch separated the audience from the actors, and members of the audience were no longer permitted to sit on stage. Recently devised lighting that consisted of lanterns and reflectors as well as candles made the back of the stage clearly visible. Scenery using flats and "drops" could represent landscapes and interiors with considerable realism.[10] But the sets were not overly elaborate and could be moved quickly, allowing for several changes of setting within a single act. Spectacles became increasingly popular in the 1770s, and Sheridan appealed to this taste in *The Critic* by his extraordinarily elaborate finale, complete with the destruction of the Spanish Armada and a procession of "all the rivers of England and their tributaries" to the sound of appropriate music.

The interest of audiences in theatrical affairs seems to have been enormous, and their power was remarkable. Riots caused by discontented theatergoers or fomented by jealous rivals were frequent. Negative reactions were expressed in intemperate articles in the newspapers and, more directly, by strident noisemakers called "catcalls" that were blown during performances. Many plays of the period were never seen again after unfavorable receptions on opening nights,[11] and Sheridan revised *The Rivals* greatly after its unsuccessful first performance. Yet the approval could also be generous. The applause at the first Author's Benefit of *She Stoops to Conquer* was said to be unequaled in its time,[12] and the clapping at the opening night of *The School for Scandal* supposedly made a passerby think that an explosion had occurred.[13]

The popularity of Goldsmith's and Sheridan's major plays increased during the nineteenth century. When they are well performed, they still delight audiences of today.

# THE PLAYS

## *The Good-Natured Man*

By the time Goldsmith wrote his first play, *The Good-Natured Man* (1768), he had already worked successfully with essays, poetry, and the novel form. His comedy shows a delight in things theatrical, as if Goldsmith could not restrain his enthusiasm for experimenting with a new medium. The play is not without awkwardness, too much plot material, and some unduly long scenes. But as the British director John Dexter recognized when he chose to revive it in 1971, it also has a great attraction—an "erratic and unpredictable humour."[1]

The play's title refers to the good-natured man much admired in the 1760s—the sentimental hero who had a great capacity for feeling and for being charitable to people in distress. Goldsmith, instead of letting his audience idealize this popular type, showed how absurd it could easily become. Modern audiences also often have a soft spot for good-hearted young men regardless of their other qualities, and so Goldsmith's ridicule is still apt today, as is his ridicule of a whole range of additional follies and foibles.

Since Goldsmith himself was good-natured to a fault, considerable self-knowledge and self-irony went into the creation of his hero. Goldsmith also drew on several literary sources. The very full characterization of George Honeywood as "the good-natured man" was probably inspired by Molière's character studies of such types as the miser, the misanthrope, and the hypocrite. Certain scenes and speeches have been traced to other French comedies.[2] But the intricate plotting is typical of English comedy, and the subplot has an English source in Steele's *The Conscious Lovers* (1722).

The first scenes of the play vividly show that George Honeywood is good-natured in all the wrong ways and is, in fact, shallow, immature, and foolish. As is revealed in the opening conversation between Sir William Honeywood, a wealthy gentleman who has just returned from abroad after a long absence, and the outspoken servant Jarvis, Sir William's nephew George, although much given to charity, often squanders his money on the undeserving. And he is emotionally so insecure that his chief concern is whether people like him, not whether they deserve his friendship.

Soon George Honeywood himself appears and confirms these reports. He is so eager to help the unfortunate that he seems not to mind having lost his money in the process. He is so bent on being kind that he is lax with his servants, who drink and steal. He is emotionally so pliable that he instantly falls in with the excessive gloom of Mr. Croaker, who is full of irrational forebodings. And he has so little self-confidence that he does nothing to win the hand of the eligible Miss Richland even though she apparently loves him.

In spite of all these flaws, however, Honeywood also

seems to have a more positive side, for Sir William, who is obviously sensible and wise, believes that his nephew has virtues that can be cultivated. We are aware from the start that it is not Honeywood's good nature, but the ways in which he misuses it, that are the problem.

The chief plot complications launched in Act I fit in perfectly with Honeywood's weaknesses. Through Sir William, a financial problem is introduced that is related to Honeywood's misplaced charity. Apparently he has lent money to an untrustworthy man who has just absconded. Sir William has acquired some incriminating papers and plans to have his nephew arrested for debt to teach him to be more careful in lending money. In addition, there are the romantic complications, introduced through Miss Richland, that are related to Honeywood's emotional unsureness. Not only does he feel unworthy of her but also, to complicate matters, he is asked by Mr. Croaker to persuade Miss Richland to accept the hand of Croaker's son Leontine. Honeywood will have to change considerably and overcome serious obstacles before he can achieve happiness.

Whereas the main plot complications prepare us for the development or the maturing of the hero, the subplot, begun at the end of Act I, introduces a web of falsehoods that will later have to be unraveled. A long conversation between Leontine and the secondary heroine Olivia reveals that Leontine was sent to France to bring home his sister, who has grown up with an aunt in Lyons, but that he has instead brought home Olivia, whom he wishes to marry. The Croaker parents are apparently unaware of the deception.

This implausible story introduces a new theme as

the young are pitted against the older generation. It also leads to two unexpectedly funny scenes of misunderstanding—situational comedy that is Goldsmith's particular forte. Forced by his strong-willed father to propose to Miss Richland, Leontine is determined to make her reject him. Miss Richland, in turn, has no interest in him, but having discovered his indifference to her, playfully decides to accept any proposal he makes. In a charming, high-spirited scene full of ironies, Leontine makes himself as unattractive as possible, inarticulately blurting out an ambiguous proposal. When Miss Richland nonetheless reacts favorably, Leontine, in an amusing reversal of tactics, suddenly displays a repelling forwardness, rushing in with declarations that are far too explicit. Meanwhile Croaker, who knows nothing of his son's love for Olivia, is exasperated and mystified by Leontine's erratic behavior.

In a second comic misunderstanding later in Act II, Croaker, misled by a report from France that the real Olivia has had an advantageous proposal, utters encouraging words to the Olivia in his household. Olivia first tries to end the pretense that she is his daughter, then assumes that Croaker approves of her marriage to Leontine. The dramatic irony reaches a high point when Leontine enters and, also assuming that his father knows the truth, kneels before him to ask his forgiveness. In the dark, as in the previous scene, Croaker is again exasperated and mystified, and the younger and older generations remain at cross-purposes.

Between these two subplot scenes, further complications are introduced with the arrival of a new character, Lofty. A busybody and influence peddler, Lofty informs Mrs. Croaker that he is helping Miss Richland with some financial problems. But his excessive name-dropping suggests that he has little influence, and so he adds to the web of falsehoods. Lofty also reveals that he, too, would like to marry Miss Richland, thereby becoming a rival of Honeywood and the reluctant Leontine.

In Act III, the focus returns to Honeywood, as Sir William's plan comes to the fore. Two bailiffs try to arrest Honeywood for debt. Bailiffs in the eighteenth century were lower class people who arrested and guarded debtors, usually in the bailiff's house, until the debt was paid. Goldsmith daringly made Mr. Timothy Twitch and Mr. Flanigan into unmistakably "low" characters, whose clumsy behavior and coarse speech are farcical in the extreme. Although Mr. Twitch has come to take Honeywood away, the sight of a dangling purse soon persuades him to guard Honeywood in his own house. Honeywood bribes the two bailiffs while they all talk high-mindedly about "the tender heart" and "humanity." Amusingly, Mr. Twitch is sufficiently familiar with the humanitarian talk of the sentimentalists to turn it to his own advantage.

The scene becomes still more amusing with the unexpected arrival of Miss Richland. Honeywood, having found some of his own clothes for the bailiffs, introduces them to Miss Richland as officer friends. Comic misunderstandings are rife as Honeywood tries to carry on a polite conversation with Miss Richland, while the bailiffs interrupt with unseemly comments of their own. The fun comes from the fact that only Honeywood, apart from the audience, knows who the two "officers" are, and he cannot explain their peculiar behavior without revealing his financial problems.

Miss Richland is baffled, and the bailiffs remain blithely unaware of the social embarrassment they are causing.

Clarifications follow this scene of confusion. Miss Richland hears from her maid who the bailiffs really are. It also becomes clear that Miss Richland, on her own, has already arranged to have Honeywood's debts repaid—a tangible sign of her interest in him. Then Sir William enters and identifies himself as Honeywood's uncle. He knows about Miss Richland's generosity and has, in turn, used his influence to settle Miss Richland's financial problems. He also warns her against Lofty, who is supposedly helping her but is not to be trusted. In this rather solemn sequence, both Sir William and Miss Richland are firmly established as equally high-minded, charitable, and clear-sighted characters.

But the laughing mood is quickly restored with the entrance of the detestable Lofty. Full of hot air and empty promises, he boasts of his friendship with Sir William, whom he visibly does not know, for he fails to recognize him. When Sir William insists that Lofty put him into touch with "Sir William," the audience has the pleasure of seeing the impudent Lofty prepare a trap for himself.

Although Honeywood's first financial problem is resolved with Miss Richland's payment of his debts, it is immediately followed by a second. Jarvis reveals that Honeywood has promised to help Leontine and Olivia elope to Scotland, where their marriage could be legalized without delay, and that, unwilling to admit he has no funds, he has given them the eighteenth-century equivalent of a worthless check. Sir William is made aware of his nephew's new foolishness and also reveals that he knows Olivia's true identity. His awareness of all the problems and his authoritative words at the end of Act III assure the audience of a final happy resolution.

Nonetheless, complications mount in Act IV. Lofty falsely tells Honeywood that he paid Honeywood's debts and persuades Honeywood to help him win Miss Richland. Honeywood continues to believe that his own love for her is hopeless. In several subsequent scenes he tries to persuade Miss Richland to marry Lofty—much to her astonishment.

The end of the play is not, however, dominated by these rather weak romantic scenes but by several brilliant scenes of farce. These are prepared as Olivia, still in Croaker's house, discovers that Honeywood's check is worthless. Her maid Garnet writes a garbled letter to Leontine asking for money, which is to be left at the Talbot Inn. Sent to get this letter to Leontine by way of Honeywood's servant, Garnet quickly returns with the news that the servant, drunk again, has dropped the letter just outside the house and that Mr. Croaker is reading it at this very moment.

The stock device of the misdelivered letter leads to the funniest scene of the play—a scene that once again is based on a major misunderstanding. Because the letter to Leontine is addressed only to "Muster Croaker," old Croaker assumes that it is meant for him. All the phrases of Garnet's garbled prose—"expedition," "being blown up," and "all of a flame"—take on a new, literal meaning. Croaker assumes that an incendiary is blackmailing him and threatening to blow him up. This unexpected joke is made plausible by Croaker's particular foible: his perpetual state of anxiety makes him leap to the wrong conclusion. He reaches the height of absurdity as he orders his house searched for combustibles and a fire engine made ready outside. While one laughs at this climax of all his fears and obtuseness, one is also aware of the poetic justice of having him suffer so intensely and unnecessarily for his foolishness.

In Act V, all the characters gather at the Talbot Inn for one more round of complications. Olivia has come to meet Leontine. Croaker arrives, expecting to find his incendiary. When Croaker explains that Honeywood has advised him to come to the inn, Leontine and Olivia wrongly assume that Honeywood has betrayed them. Only the audience knows that they are all there because Garnet's letter referred to the Talbot Inn.

A farcical scene of mistaken identities follows. In search of the supposed incendiary, the postboy drags in the faithful Jarvis. Then Croaker pounces on the postboy, whom he takes for the incendiary. Honeywood, who has just arrived, tries to clarify matters, but no one will listen to him. Indeed, in an amusing reversal of the treatment usually accorded to the hero in the last act, all the assembled company— Olivia, Leontine, Croaker, Jarvis, and even the postboy—turn on Honeywood and blame him for interfering with their lives.

The moment has now come for unraveling the various falsehoods. Olivia finally explains to Croaker that she is not his daughter, and Croaker accepts her as his future daughter-in-law instead. Honeywood has a much-needed moment of insight and realizes that he has "overtaxed" his means in trying to help Olivia and Leontine. Lofty, after once more spouting the names of nonexistent influential friends, is unmasked as a sham, for Sir William reveals his true identity.

When Sir William reveals himself, the stage directions read "Discovering his ensign of the Bath"; that is, showing the insignia of the Order of the Bath, the honorary society to which an English monarch appoints a few chosen noblemen. With this aristocratic gesture, Sir William appears almost godlike—a *deus ex machina* of classical drama come to help with the unraveling. In this guise Sir William not only shames Lofty but also pronounces judgment on Honeywood:

> I saw with regret those splendid errors, that still took name from some neighbouring duty. Your charity, that was but injustice; your benevolence, that was but weakness; and your friendship but credulity.

Miss Richland is finally revealed as Honeywood's real benefactor, and Honeywood realizes that Miss Richland is prepared to marry him. He also recognizes that he must reserve his pity, friendship, and benevolence for those who deserve it. At the end the two plot strands of unmasking and maturing are brought neatly together as Honeywood learns to see through false friends and recognize the true.

The characters involved in this extraordinarily varied and complicated plot are, visibly, types. They make an oddly assorted cast, perhaps because they are derived from many different kinds of comedy. Still, several are remarkably vivid, and some have amusing foibles or quirks that show Goldsmith's special insight into human nature.

George Honeywood is obviously an exaggerated version of the sentimental hero. His very name is ambiguous, suggesting the sweetness of the man of feeling and, at the same time, a "would-be" quality that implies a falling short of the ideal. It may seem strange that as the central figure of the comedy he has no vivid traits—only a lack of self-assurance, a lack of discernment, a lack of good sense. One critic has bluntly called him "an ass."[3] But he is a type that goes back as far as Roman comedy—the immature, rather helpless young man without pronounced personality known as the *adulescens*.[4]

Honeywood's vapidity emphasizes the point Goldsmith set out to make in his play, that one should not thoughtlessly idealize the good-natured man. In fact, the characterization of Honeywood is in keeping with the ideas Goldsmith was later to express in his "Essay on the Theatre," in which he objected to the audience's tendency to condone any faults in the sentimental hero merely because he has a good heart.[5] Honeywood's faults are never condoned, and he has to recognize them fully before he is made happy.

In obvious contrast to Honeywood is his intended bride, Miss Richland. Her name suggests only that she has a fortune, but she is actually high-spirited and clever, with intellectual interests that extend, oddly enough, to French literary criticism. She is chiefly important, however, for her good sense and self-assurance, combined with a genuine capacity for love and a reasonable charity—all positive qualities that correspond to Honeywood's failings. Clearly, she represents Goldsmith's own ideals. And, interestingly, she has a much stronger personality than Honeywood, thereby prefiguring Kate Hardcastle in *She Stoops to Conquer*, who is also more dominant than the young hero of the play.

Leontine and Olivia are more conventional lovers than the principal couple, and theirs is the more conventional problem of having to overcome a father's opposition rather than their own or their partner's weaknesses. Yet Leontine is amusing in that he thinks himself so clever as he begins his insincere courtship of Miss Richland, only to find himself outwitted at his own game.

Much more memorable than the young lovers is the play's chief father figure, Croaker. His very name suggests the raven, that bird of ill omen, and his first entrance is heralded by a series of amusingly exaggerated death images. He is the eternal pessimist, who obviously relishes his lugubriousness. "Ah, my dear friend," he exclaims to Honeywood in their first scene, "it is a perfect satisfaction to be miserable with you." For most of the play, Croaker seems outrageously absurd, looming larger than life. But at the end, when he is quickly reconciled to the match between his son and Olivia, he becomes more human and shows an unexpected inconsistency. "There's the advantage of fretting away our misfortunes beforehand," he explains; "we never feel them when they come." He illustrates the paradox that a man who always broods about impending calamities may have used up his capacity for pain by the time disaster strikes.

Goldsmith acknowledged that he modeled Croaker on the figure of Suspirius in Dr. Samuel Johnson's *Rambler*, No. 59,[6] who sheds gloom wherever he goes. But even more, Croaker is the sort of character one finds in Ben Jonson's comedies, characters in whom one "humor" or dominant passion has warped the entire personality. And, in addition, he is the easily exasperated, choleric father, a popular figure going back as far as Roman comedy.

Whereas Croaker is a psychological type, Lofty, the

play's second remarkably vivid character, is a social type. Lofty's name suggests the elevated social spheres in which he wishes to move as well as the heights of pretense from which he eventually tumbles. Exuding vanity and hypocrisy, he struts about, accompanied by a foppish French servant, and invariably gives a dazzling display of name-dropping. Although some of his lines are known to be direct borrowings from a French comedy,[7] he is also inspired at least partly by the vain and hypocritical fops or fools of late seventeenth-century English comedy.

In sharp contrast to all the other characters, who belong roughly to the same social sphere, the bailiffs represent the lower classes. They add a touch of earthiness and a reminder of what real poverty is like. At the same time, they are just rascally enough in their acceptance of Honeywood's bribe and grotesque enough in their speech and manners to remain thoroughly comic figures.

The bailiffs were probably suggested by the low, clownish characters in Shakespeare's comedies. They were found so shocking by the original audience that they were cut from almost all the performances.[8] But Goldsmith rightly reintroduced them in his printed text and expressed the hope, in his preface, "that too much refinement will not banish humour and character" from the stage.

Sir William Honeywood, finally, is the wise older man who sees, controls, and judges everyone from start to finish. Twice he describes himself as a "concealed spectator" of Honeywood's follies (Acts I and II), and he might have said the same regarding the other characters. He is genuinely helpful to the deserving and properly critical of the foolish. Although he is generous, he is also prudent and discriminating.

In being a "concealed spectator," judge, and kindly uncle all in one, Sir William is supposed to be entirely admirable. He recalls the dukes of Shakespeare's comedies quite as much as the *deus ex machina* of classical drama. He can even be seen as the human image of the benign deity accepted in the eighteenth century, the "concealed spectator" of all man's follies, who tests man, makes him see the truth, and provides a happy ending once it is earned. And yet, for modern audiences, Goldsmith's spokesman for true, controlled benevolence is too uniformly in the right. He is too "straight," too good, to be quite believable.

All the characters are carefully related to each other by parallels and contrasts. There are two pairs of lovers, one confronted with psychological and the other with external obstacles. One of the young men is timid and ineffectual, the other relatively self-assured; one of the young women is high-spirited, the other melancholy. The two father-figures differ in that Sir William is benevolent and even-tempered; Mr. Croaker, mercenary and obstinate. The Croakers, as a couple, are striking opposites: Mrs. Croaker is always ready to laugh, while Mr. Croaker spreads his gloom. Such pairing and contrasting of characters have been characteristic of comedy since the plays of Plautus and Terence.

But the play is not as neat and tidy as these parallels and contrasts suggest. It is full of surprises, not the least of which come from its remarkably varied tone. This ranges from outright scorn for Honeywood and Lofty, to warm approbation for Sir William. In addition, there is occasionally a good-humored acceptance of human quirks or oddities of behavior: not only of Croaker's various foibles but also of Twitch's unexpected argumentativeness (Act III) and even of Jarvis's understandable inconsistency as he cannot bear having others criticize his master even though he feels quite free to criticize him himself (Act V). Such benign humor was typical of the earlier *Vicar of Wakefield* and was to become even more dominant in *She Stoops to Conquer*, of which it is, in fact, one of the most memorable features.

The style of *The Good-Natured Man* has quite as much variety and range as the tone. Before Goldsmith turned to drama, he was already an accomplished prose stylist, known for his "middle style"—something between the very colloquial, on the one hand, and the very ornate on the other.[9] What is remarkable in the style of his first comedy, however, is the avoidance of a uniform prose style and the experimenting with different styles to suit the various characters.

Particularly memorable, for instance, are the blunt and blustering speeches of old Croaker. In answer to Leontine, who does not want to court Miss Richland and pleads: "But, Sir, if you will but listen to reason—" Croaker retorts: "Come, then, produce your reasons. I tell you I'm fix'd, determined, so now produce your reasons. When I'm determined, I always listen to reason because it can then do no harm" (Act I). His answer sounds plain and vigorous, but it is also full of unconscious irony.

Mrs. Croaker and Lofty speak in a more elaborate style, using witty balance or contrasts. Describing a recent auction, Mrs. Croaker gossips about "the deaf dowager, as usual, bidding like fury against herself. And then so curious in antiques! Herself the most genuine piece of antiquity in the whole collection" (Act I). Lofty, when unmasked, declares: "So then my confounded genius has been all this time leading me only up to the garret, in order to fling me out of the window" (Act V). Very concise, these lines are still close to natural speech and communicate easily from the stage.

Goldsmith's versatility extends to the cleverly ambiguous statements with double meanings in the Olivia-Croaker scene of Act II and the "incendiary letter." The verbal high point of the play, however, comes in the bailiff scene, in which Miss Richland's elegant, learned remarks are juxtaposed with the coarse, chauvinistic outbursts of Twitch and Flanigan, and in which double meanings again abound.

> MISS RICH: Yet, Mr. Honeywood, this does not convince me but that severity in criticism is necessary. It was our first adopting the severity of French taste, that has brought them in turn to taste us.
>
> BAILIFF: Taste us! By the Lord, Madam, they devour us. Give Monseers but a taste, and I'll be damn'd, but they come in for a bellyful.
>
> MISS RICH: Very extraordinary this.
>
> FOLLOWER: But very true. What makes the bread rising, the parle vous that devour us. What makes the mutton fivepence a pound, the parle vous that eat it up. What makes the beer three pence halfpenny the pot—

This scene has been rightly likened to the afternoon tea scene in George Bernard Shaw's *Pygmalion*,[10] for the references to the French as "parle vous," the crass mention of mutton and pence, and the use of "bellyful" must have been as shocking to Goldsmith's audience as Eliza Doolittle's salty talk was to Shaw's.

Although much of *The Good-Natured Man* is time-less fun, some of the details take on added significance when they are recognized as specific parodies of the sentimentalism popular in Goldsmith's time. For instance, the long sigh that Honeywood utters after his first interview with Croaker (Act I) is a takeoff on the usual signs of sentiment, such as tears, with which a sentimental hero was supposed to respond to the woes of the world. Croaker's brooding over pain and suffering is also a variation of sentimental melancholy. When Twitch talks about his "tender heart" for his own mercenary purposes (Act III) and when Lofty, pretending to be Honeywood's benefactor, exclaims "Blood, sir, can't a man be permitted to enjoy the luxury of his own feeling without all this parade?" (Act IV), their speeches parody the high-minded verbiage of sentimentalism. Even Leontine is repeatedly placed into situations that parody the conventional scenes of sentimental comedy: proposals made by bashful or effusive lovers, the kneeling of erring sons who beg their fathers for forgiveness. In Goldsmith, all these shows of sentiment are either false and hypocritical or unwarranted by the occasion, and they call not for sympathy but for laughter.

Still, it is obvious that Goldsmith is mocking various kinds of facile sentimentalism, not sentiment as such. As we have seen, he consistently upholds genuine sentiment—the capacity for love and charity—provided that it is checked by good sense, prudence, and discrimination. In short, Goldsmith is enough a man of his time to value the good heart and enough a critic of his time to insist that it be balanced by a clear head.

As a whole, the play expresses Goldsmith's essentially conservative view of life. The established hierarchy is

Goldsmith's odd characters with their distinctive follies or
foibles were vividly recreated in the 1971 National Theatre
production of *The Good-Natured Man.* Here the irrepressible name-dropper Lofty (James Dale) is trying to
impress the sprightly heroine, Miss Richland (Maureen
Lipton), while the lugubrious Mr. Croaker (Bill Fraser)
and the sensible Sir William look on.

affirmed both within the family and within the larger society. It is significant that the young, with the exception of Miss Richland, are immature and foolish. Some of the older people, notably Croaker and Lofty, are also foolish, but Sir William, the head of the Honeywood family and the most aristocratic member of society, is wise. The young and foolish must come up to the established standards represented by this older and wiser man.

On the stage, Goldsmith's lively though somewhat uneven first comedy has had only limited success. It was not easy for Goldsmith to have it produced in the first place. His acquaintance David Garrick, then manager of the Theatre Royal in Drury Lane, to whom he submitted the play in summer 1767, asked for so many revisions and then so delayed his acceptance that Goldsmith submitted it instead to George Coleman, manager of the Theatre Royal in Covent Garden. To make matters worse, Garrick then accepted Hugh Kelly's *False Delicacy*, written in the same vein as *The Good-Natured Man* in partly ridiculing excessive sentiment but more to the contemporary audience's taste in also capitalizing on the sentimental mood. After further delay by Coleman, *The Good-Natured Man* was finally performed on January 29, 1768. It had a limited run of eleven performances in 1768 and only two further performances in Goldsmith's lifetime, in 1771 and 1773. The bailiff scene was dropped after being hissed the first night but was restored in the 1773 production.[11]

Performances after the eighteenth century were rare. Programs have survived from productions in 1826 and 1881 in London, and 1916 in Birmingham. A New York production of 1870 featured George Clarke as Honeywood, Fanny Davenport as Miss Richland, and Mrs. Gilbert as Mrs. Croaker. Thereafter, the play survived in America only in college productions: the Yale Dramatic Company's of 1903 and the Amherst Masquers' of 1931, directed by Curtis Canfield.[12]

Two English directors did, however, become interested in the play in the twentieth century. In 1939, Tyrone Guthrie organized a production for the Old Vic in which Robert Donat played Croaker; Stewart Granger, Honeywood; and Constance Neville, Miss Richland. The company played in several suburban theaters, but the coming of World War II cut short the run. John Dexter directed the first successful modern revival for the National Theatre in 1971. As might have been expected, Croaker and Lofty dominated the play. One reviewer wrote approvingly of "Bill Fraser's Croaker, an inconsolable Walrus, raking the theatre with his huge, absurdly sorrowful eyes," and of Jim Dale's Lofty, "like Bugs Bunny in a wig extravagantly powdered, trailing his legs behind him like a dying doll."[13] Desmond McNamara as Honeywood and Maureen Lipton as Miss Richland both wore rimless glasses, presumably to suggest their affinity with young people of the 1970s.

John Dexter set out to "catch that streak of eccentric laughter and character"[14] in Goldsmith's first comedy and was indeed able to prove that it has more to offer on the stage than is generally recognized.

## She Stoops to Conquer

One of the most popular comedies of the English-speaking world, *She Stoops to Conquer* (1773) is memorable for its gaiety, liveliness, and innocent fun. Modern critics have praised it for its "robustness," its "horseplay and sentiment."[1] Dr. Samuel Johnson well described its appeal at the time of its first production: "I know of no comedy for many years that has so much exhilarated an audience, that has answered so much the great end of comedy—making an audience merry."[2]

As the subtitle "Mistakes of the Night" suggests, Goldsmith delighted in misunderstandings that have far-reaching ramifications. His plot seems to have been based on a mistake he himself supposedly made in his youth, when he took a prosperous squire's house for an inn.[3] Combining this incident with traditional comedy material, such as mistaken identity and pairs of lovers in conflict with their parents or guardians, he created a highly intricate plot that permitted a wide range of comic scenes, from farce to high comedy. Indeed, in keeping with the ideas he had just expressed in his "Essay on the Theatre; or, A Comparison Between Laughing and Sentimental Comedy"[4] (1773), Goldsmith made his play as funny as possible, moving swiftly from one hilarious scene to the next. And all the while he vividly revealed the very human foibles or follies of his characters.

The opening scene, focusing on the Hardcastle family in their comfortable house in the country, shows Goldsmith's masterly sense of how to prepare for a joke. Mrs. Hardcastle complains that the rambling house "looks for all the world like an inn." A doting mother, she makes excuses for Tony Lumpkin, her son by a previous marriage, who is much given to practical jokes. Then the heroine, Kate Hardcastle, appears in fashionable clothes, a sign of her two-year stay in London, but indicates that she will soon change into a simpler dress to please her father.

This opening not only prepares for many later complications but also immediately asks the audience to judge the values of the characters. Mrs. Hardcastle is obviously foolish, especially in her longing to be in London. Tony Lumpkin, who appears briefly, praising the alehouse, contradicting his mother, and dragging her off stage, is crude and has lived too long in the country. Mr. Hardcastle, in contrast, is wise enough to distrust the "vanity and affectation" of the town and educated enough to avoid the uncouthness of the country. Kate, like her father, also seems capable of moderation, and her alternative ways of dressing raise questions about the values of town and country life.

Soon two romantic intrigues are set into motion. Mr. Hardcastle announces to Kate that the young man he has chosen to be her husband will arrive shortly. Marlow sounds like a paragon except for one disturb-

ing trait, an inexplicable shyness. Then Constance
Neville, Mrs. Hardcastle's niece and also a member of
the household, admits to Kate that she has an admirer,
Mr. Hastings, who is a friend of Marlow's. To complicate matters, Mrs. Hardcastle, who has control over
Constance's fortune, wants her to marry Tony Lumpkin to keep the money in the family.

The middle of Act I brings a radical change in mood
as the scene shifts to "The Three Pigeons," the local
alehouse, where Tony offers a raucous song to the
approval of his noisy friends. This moment of farce is
followed by the arrival of two young strangers—
Marlow and Hastings. They do not know where they
are, and so Tony has a chance to play one of his
practical jokes. Claiming to send them to "the old
Buck's Head on the hill, one of the best inns in the
whole country," he directs them to Mr. Hardcastle's
house.

Act II begins with another moment of farce as Mr.
Hardcastle tries in vain to teach his rough country
servants how to serve dinner to the expected guests.
The scene stands in an amusing contrast to the next, in
which the elegant Marlow and Hastings arrive. Pre-
dictably, the young men take their voluble host for
the innkeeper and arrogantly order him about.

Marlow's first scene on stage reveals that he has an
odd personality problem that will intensify the confusion caused by Tony's joke. He is terrified of well-bred
women, although he has no difficulties with "females
of another class." His shyness—certainly an absurd
foible for a young man of the town—is soon demon-
strated, for when he is introduced to Miss Hardcastle,
he is so timid that he cannot even raise his eyes to her
face.

This first meeting between the two young people is delightful for its presentation of social embarrassment as well as for the unexpected reversal of male and female roles. Marlow is absurdly callow and inept, making conversation with Miss Hardcastle by uttering inane, high-minded generalities. As he bumbles on, Kate takes over and completes his phrases with grace and assurance. Their exchange parodies the standard genteel conversation of sentimental lovers— a point that is emphasized when Kate laughingly exclaims at the end of the scene, "Was there ever such a sober sentimental interview?" But the fun of the scene comes chiefly from the excruciating ineffectuality of the previously arrogant young man.

Immediately following this scene, Hastings meets Constance Neville and discovers that he is in the Hardcastle house. The two decide to elope as soon as they can lay their hands on Constance's jewels. In a lively sequence of social comedy mingled with farce, Hastings outrageously flatters the vain Mrs. Hardcastle to lull her suspicions, while Constance flirts with the reluctant Tony Lumpkin. By the end of Act II, Tony has discovered Hastings' interest in Constance and offers his help, even to the extent of procuring the jewels.

In Act III, the main and subplots reach their point of greatest complication in some of the funniest scenes of the play. The stock device of stolen jewels creates a series of dazzling reversals and surprises. First Tony gives Hastings Constance's jewels, which he has stolen from his mother. Then Mrs. Hardcastle refuses to give Constance the jewels, claiming that they are lost. Next, Mrs. Hardcastle finds that they are really gone. While she complains bitterly, Tony, with his usual love of practical jokes, pretends to think that she is merely playacting. And while she thinks Tony a fool, he greatly enjoys making a fool of her.

The focus returns to the main plot, as Kate discovers Marlow's mistake about the house and also finds that he has seen her in her simple country dress and believes she is the inn's barmaid. Playfully, she decides to continue in this lowly role. A second interview between the two young people, which parallels and contrasts with their first, shows Marlow's other side to Kate.

Unlike the preceding jewel scene that borders on farce, the Kate-Marlow scene is high comedy at its best—sophisticated, with sparkling verbal exchanges and a great deal of irony derived from what each of the two pretends to be and thinks or knows about the other. While Kate tries to catch his attention, Marlow thinks aloud about the Miss Hardcastle he met earlier, whom he now considers "too grave and sentimental" and to whom he attributes a squint. Then, looking Kate squarely in the face for the first time, he finds the supposed barmaid "vastly handsome" and comments on her "sprightly malicious eye" (in amusing contrast to the squint he has just attributed to *his* Miss Hardcastle). In a snappy interchange, Marlow proudly asserts his superiority over a mere barmaid, unaware that she is leading him on.

The high comedy intensifies as Marlow tries to come closer to Kate by pretending to guess her age, and she fends him off with a witty reply that is also appropriate to her role of country barmaid: "Pray, Sir, keep your distance. One would think you wanted to know one's age as they do horses, by mark of mouth." Obviously enjoying the game, Kate next leads Marlow to talk about his Miss Hardcastle. The ironies increase as he describes Miss Hardcastle's supposed short-comings, his own prowess in dealing with her, and even his imaginary successes with various ladies in town. The scene ends on a high point as Marlow becomes still more familiar, tries to take her hand, and begins to pull her about—to the surprise of the enter-ing Mr. Hardcastle. However, in a brief interview following Marlow's hurried exit, Kate promises to convince her father that Marlow is not as impudent as Mr. Hardcastle believes.

Act IV brings the jewel complications to a surpris-ing end. We gather that Hastings has given the jewels to Marlow for safekeeping and that Marlow, in turn, has given them to the supposed landlady. In a delight-fully underplayed moment, Hastings merely shows pained surprise, which he cannot explain to Marlow, at the news that the jewels are back in Mrs. Hard-castle's hands.

Next, the Marlow-Mr. Hardcastle complication comes to a head as Mr. Hardcastle, finding both Marlow's rudeness and the crude behavior of his servants unbearable, orders Marlow out of his house. For the first time the young man dimly realizes that all is not what it seems, and the unraveling begins. Ironically, Marlow turns to the supposed barmaid for reassurance and learns that he is in Mr. Hardcastle's house. This revelation is coupled with a moment of insight that confirms Kate's good opinion of him. For Marlow realizes how he must have appeared to his host: "What a swaggering puppy must he take me for. What a silly puppy do I find myself." But the revelation is far from complete, for Kate, instead of disclosing her own identity, now pretends to be a poor relation in the Hardcastle house.

This further ruse of Kate's becomes a test of Marlow's character. When the embarrassed Marlow talks of leaving immediately, Kate begins to cry, and Marlow is touched by the fact that, for the first time in his life, "a modest woman" has shown signs of affection for him. But he is faced with the dilemma that the girl in front of him is too poor to be an acceptable wife, yet too good to be merely seduced. To modern audiences, Marlow's class consciousness is hard to accept, but Goldsmith was a man of his time, and so he lets Kate find Marlow "generous" and admirable.

The revelation experienced by Marlow is followed by another involving Mrs. Hardcastle. In her presence Tony receives a letter from Hastings. Since Tony is illiterate and Constance suspects that the letter may deal with her planned elopement, she volunteers to read it aloud. But instead of reading the actual text, she fabricates one. The ruse works for only a short time before Mrs. Hardcastle reads Hastings's actual letter, and the proposed elopement comes to light.

With these various revelations, most of the young people are brought to their low point. Mrs. Hardcastle plans to take Constance to her feared Aunt Pedigree, from whom no escape is possible. Hastings despairs of ever being united with Constance. Marlow is desperately embarrassed about his mistake. Marlow and Hastings fall to blaming each other and turn on Tony Lumpkin as well. Still, Act IV ends on a more positive note, for Tony promises to show that he is "a more good-natured fellow" than they think.

The arrival of Marlow's father, Sir Charles, at the

beginning of Act V brings further misunderstandings. The two parents, eager to bring about the union of their children, hear Marlow claim that he hardly knows Miss Hardcastle and then Kate, in a separate interview, declare that Marlow knows her well. Ironically, both are telling the truth from their points of view. Then Kate arranges to have the two fathers hide behind a screen in half an hour's time to hear Marlow profess his love.

This main action is interrupted by a new scene of farce. Hastings meets Tony in the garden and hears that Tony has played yet another practical joke. Instead of taking his mother and Constance to Aunt Pedigree's house miles away, he has led them through every bog and fen within a short radius of the Hardcastle house, finally depositing them in a horsepond on their own grounds. Tony's vivid description, a comic analogue to the Greek messenger's narration of catastrophes that cannot easily be shown on stage, suggests the discomforts of the ride:

> I first took them down Feather-bed-lane, where we stuck fast in the mud. I then rattled them crack over the stones of Up-and-down Hill—I then introduced them to the gibbet on Heavytree Heath, and from that, with a circumbendibus, I fairly lodged them in the horsepond at the bottom of the garden.
>
> (ACT V, P. 203)

The entrance of the mud-spattered and badly frightened Mrs. Hardcastle confirms the impression that she has been led a terrible chase.

The farce intensifies as Tony, seeing Mr. Hardcastle, thinks of new mischief and pretends that Hardcastle is a highwayman. As Mrs. Hardcastle first cowers behind a tree and then abases herself before the supposed highwayman, really her husband, she reaches a well-deserved low point of her own.

Finally the moment comes for the long-expected recognition scene between Marlow and Kate. The young man wishes to take his leave, still thinking of Kate as a poor relation in the house. When he hears her talk modestly about herself and realistically about his need to marry a woman of fortune, he melts. Just as Mr. Hardcastle and Sir Charles take their places behind the screen, Marlow declares Kate's lack of fortune irrelevant and expresses his love:

> Your beauty first caught my eye; for who could see that without emotion. But every moment that I converse with you, steals in some new grace, heightens the picture, and gives it stronger expression. What at first seem'd rustic plainness, now appears refin'd simplicity. What seem'd forward assurance, now strikes me as the result of courageous innocence and conscious virtue.

With this eloquent description, Marlow completes the test of his character. For the first time he recognizes Kate for what she is, and for the first time, too, he trusts his feelings.

Marlow's declaration provides a brief moment of sentiment necessary to complete the romantic complications. But soon the fathers emerge from their hiding and reproach Marlow for pretending hardly to know Miss Hardcastle. Only when Hardcastle refers to his daughter does the full truth dawn on Marlow:

> MARLOW: Daughter!—this lady your daughter!
> HARDCASTLE: Yes, Sir, my only daughter. My

Kate, whose else should she be.
MARLOW: Oh, the devil.

After this delightfully understated moment of insight, Kate is allowed to tease Marlow for his earlier behavior. The young man is just embarrassed enough to pay for his earlier foolishness but not so humiliated as to put his reconciliation with the Hardcastles in doubt.

Only the fate of Constance and her Hastings remains to be determined. They arrive to claim Constance's fortune and appeal to Mr. Hardcastle for help. In a surprise turn, Mr. Hardcastle reveals that Tony Lumpkin is actually of age and under no obligation to follow his mother's orders to marry Constance. Reversing the wedding vows one expects to hear at the end of a comedy, Tony solemnly *refuses* to take Constance "for my true and lawful wife," leaving her free to marry Hastings. Kate and Marlow are also ready to become united, and Mr. Hardcastle, joining their hands, plans the appropriate wedding feast so that "the Mistakes of the Night shall be crowned with a merry morning."

The characters involved in all the fun and games have, for the most part, rich and attractive personalities. They move quite naturally through the intrigue, seemingly just being themselves, and often some particular character trait brings about the implausible happenings in seemingly natural ways. Indeed, its naturalness has been cited as one of the key strengths of the play.[5]

Yet this naturalness is the result of art that conceals art. The characters are still rooted in traditional comic types. These types are, however, humanized by Goldsmith's distinctive sense of humor, his liking for foibles and idiosyncrasies. And the characterization is enriched by the continuous testing and judging of everyone's values—of strengths and weaknesses and very ways of life.

Marlow is the perennial immature young man, overbearing on some occasions and unsure of himself on others. His special foible of being bold with one kind of woman and shy with another may strike us as strange but can be explained by the typical English upbringing: aristocratic young men were until recently brought up by servants, not mothers, and were consequently often more at ease with lower class than upper class women. Marlow's foible becomes a splendid plot device, motivating his inhibitions with his intended fiancée and his enthusiasm for the same young woman disguised as a barmaid.

The character of Marlow is an amusing composite of literary types. As an attractive but immature and slightly helpless lover, he belongs to the unformed young heroes who go back to the *adulescens* of Roman comedy.[6] In his odd duality in relation to women, he also belongs to a type known as the "double gallant"—a young man modest with some women but a rake with others—that had been successful in a number of eighteenth-century comedies.[7] And in his extreme shyness he is a parody of the sentimental hero, in whom bashfulness was regarded as a sign of admirable sensitivity. True to his antisentimental position in *The Good-Natured Man* and "An Essay on the Theatre," Goldsmith makes such bashfulness a sign of his hero's immaturity and lets him suffer repeated embarrassments as well as several moments of painful insight before he can win the heroine.

Kate Hardcastle is one of Goldsmith's most delightful creations. She unites within herself a series of contrasting qualities: wit and warmth, self-possession and feeling for others, knowledge of the world and innocence. When Marlow eventually sees her for what she is, he quite properly praises her for her "refined simplicity" (Act V), a studied simplicity that avoids both the undesirable affectations associated with the town and the undue "rustic plainness" typical of the country. It is difficult to make such balance and moderation vivid, but Kate emerges as a refreshingly harmonious figure who combines the best of the town and the country, head and heart, without losing her sparkle and spunk.

High-spirited and strong-minded, Kate belongs to the tradition of sprightly Shakespearean heroines such as Rosalind of *As You Like It* and Viola of *Twelfth Night*. In thoroughly enjoying her ruses, wordplay included, to fool young Marlow, she is also a descendant of the witty and self-possessed heroines of late seventeenth-century comedies. The irony of her behavior—her playful and witty lowering of herself to win her suitor—is emphasized by the paradoxical title phrase "she stoops to conquer."

The play's second pair of lovers is more conventional. Hastings is the polished young man of the town, who, unlike his friend Marlow, knows how to behave in society. Constance Neville is the universal type of sensible young woman. Both are more worldly than Marlow. They have practical, realistic concerns about securing Constance's fortune, recognizing that money is necessary to maintain oneself in society.

Far more vivid and complex is the irrepressible Tony Lumpkin. As representative of the country, he is indeed "lumpish" and crude. Yet his good nature,

energy and earthiness emerge as attractive and important aspects of human nature. His particular foible, a
liking for practical jokes, is fully appropriate to his
rustic character and makes him, as one critic has
pointed out, more "an imp" than "an oaf."[8] Tony's
practical jokes are then ingeniously used to bring about
most of the complications—not only the mistaking of
the house for an inn but also the jewel theft and Mrs.
Hardcastle's harrowing ride through bog and fen.

Tony Lumpkin was undoubtedly inspired by the
country booby type popular in English social comedies from the late seventeenth century on. There is,
however, an amusing reversal of the usual treatment
of this type. For whereas country boobies were invariably made the butt of jokes played by witty and
polished members of town society, it is Marlow and
Hastings, fresh from London, and Mrs. Hardcastle
with her townish pretensions who become the butt of
Tony Lumpkin's jokes.

Mrs. Hardcastle is another familiar type: the older
woman full of unseemly vanity and affectation. This
type, usually shown in a town environment in English
social comedies, becomes even funnier when transposed to the country, where longings to be fashionable seem all the more absurd. Mrs. Hardcastle is also
the universal type of a blindly doting mother. Utterly
foolish as well as selfish and mercenary, she fully deserves the tricks that are played on her.

Mr. Hardcastle is a richer composite of types. One
of the best-rounded figures of the play, he is endowed
with several foibles that help to make the far-fetched
happenings plausible. A country squire by choice as
well as social position, he has a bluffness and studied
plainness of manner that account for his being mis-

taken for an innkeeper. A crotchety and opinionated older man, he expects the young to behave badly
and therefore does not question Marlow's arrogance.[9]
At the same time, however, Mr. Hardcastle is an
appealing father figure, who can be kindly and genial
when not irritated. He is endowed with Goldsmith's
own quirky sense of humor, as seen in the curious
compromise plan for Kate's dress. This odd sense of
humor is used in the service of common sense, for
Mr. Hardcastle is trying to teach Kate the values of
a simple life.

Clearly, Mr. Hardcastle, like Kate, represents the
ideal values of the play, especially good sense and
affection when it is warranted. He also has an admirable appreciation for permanence as opposed to shifting
fashions, best seen in his praise of "every thing that's
old: old friends, old times, old manners, old books, old
wine" and even "an old wife" (Act I). He is a plausible spokesman for Goldsmith's values because he is not
himself perfect but remains a comic figure with foibles
of his own.

The servants in the Hardcastle household, along with
Tony Lumpkin's drinking companions, are low figures
probably modeled on Shakespeare's clowns.[10] They
are much funnier on stage than they appear from a
mere reading of the play, for they give the actors the
opportunity to improvise. They also serve as an ironic
comment on the social pretensions of some of the
more polished characters.

All these diverse characters are assembled with a
keen sense of parallels and contrasts. The pairs of
lovers and their parents have sharply contrasting personalities and problems. The hero is weaker than the
heroine, and both are confronted with his curious

psychological problem. The secondary lovers are more evenly matched and have to deal with the more conventional problem of a guardian's opposition. The parents, Mr. and Mrs. Hardcastle, have strongly contrasting tastes and values. A further contrast is introduced between representatives of the town—Marlow and Hastings—and of the country—Tony Lumpkin. Such parallels and contrasts, in the tradition of Roman and Elizabethan comedy, help to give shape to the whole.

But it is chiefly Goldsmith's cheerful, genial tone and all-pervasive sense of humor that unify the play. Not only does Goldsmith have a particularly English, or perhaps Irish, sense of humor in his liking for homely tricks and jokes that make a canny point. He also has "a sense of humor" in the most fundamental meaning of the phrase: he sees the absurdities in human nature and accepts them as an intriguing part of life. Relishing idiosyncrasies of character as well as the odd ways in which character and situations can mesh, he treats most of his figures with benign amusement. There is almost no sharp satire except of Mrs. Hardcastle and her affectations. For the rest, Goldsmith accepts their follies or foibles as part of human nature and seems to be affirming throughout the play that life in all its peculiarity is good. Rooted in common sense and common experience, his humor is relaxed and mellow.

The style contributes greatly to the humor and also to the naturalness of the play. Most of the dialogue is close to normal speech and sounds natural even to twentieth-century ears. At his best, Goldsmith achieves a delightful, colloquial freshness, as, for instance, in the early scene in which Marlow and Hastings look over what they take to be the inn's menu and arrogantly order dinner from the astonished Mr. Hardcastle:

> MARLOW: (Reading) For the first course at the top, a pig, and pruin [prune] sauce.
> HASTINGS: Damn your pig, I say.
> MARLOW: And damn your pruin sauce, say I.
> HARDCASTLE: And yet, gentlemen, to men that are hungry, pig, with pruin sauce, is very good eating.
> MARLOW: At the bottom, a calve's tongue and brains.
> HASTINGS: Let your brains be knock'd out, my good Sir; I don't like them.
> MARLOW: Or you may clap them on a plate by themselves. I do.
> HARDCASTLE: (Aside) Their impudence confounds me. (To them) Gentlemen, you are my guests, make what alterations you please.
>
> (ACT II)

The very specific culinary details, the colloquial diction, and the abruptness of the young men's replies intensify the dramatic irony of the moment.

Tony Lumpkin's speeches are more colloquial still, especially when he describes Constance to Hastings as "a cantanckerous toad," capable of "as many tricks as a hare in a thicket," and "as loud as a hog in a gate" (Act II). These animal images, although they are not appropriate for the young woman being described, well fit the rustic Tony.

The dialogue in the Kate-Marlow scenes modulates from the rather elevated, when Marlow addresses Miss Hardcastle, to the direct and colloquial, when he speaks to the barmaid. The fun of the barmaid scenes is increased on the stage because Kate's speeches are usually played with a broad Yorkshire accent, which is dropped imperceptibly as the moment of recognition approaches. Goldsmith's style is, in short, unobtrusively varied and versatile, and contributes greatly to the laughing mood.

In countless ways, then, Goldsmith succeeded in creating a "laughing comedy" as an antidote to the sentimental comedies popular in his day. He consciously avoided high-minded, lachrymose scenes and the uniformly genteel tone of sentimental comedy, introducing many hilarious scenes, horseplay, and clownish characters. Even the one solemn moment when Marlow fully recognizes the qualities of the heroine is undercut by the dramatic irony of having two irate fathers behind the screen.

Yet the values upheld in the play are not untouched by the cult of sentiment. Clearly, the heart is valued, for Marlow is rewarded as soon as he trusts his feelings, and both Kate and Mr. Hardcastle have a great capacity for feeling. Furthermore, nearly all of the characters are basically good: Marlow has "the virtues that will improve with age" (Act III), and Tony Lumpkin is "a good-natured fellow" at heart. In addition, the country—the setting of all the exhilarating happenings—is made preferable to the town.

Still, at bottom, what is extolled is no single ideal but rather a balance of qualities. Significantly, Marlow's rush of feeling at the end is offset by Constance's concern for her fortune: the claims of both sentiment and prudence are recognized. On the question of whether life in the country or in town is preferable—really a metaphor for which set of values is preferable—the play suggests a middle course—an attractive ideal that avoids the worst and combines the best that country and town have to offer. It is "refined simplicity," a quality not only of Kate's character but also of Mr. Hardcastle's very way of life. In short, the play celebrates the time-honored values of good nature checked by good sense and moderation.

The play reflects a conservative point of view in other respects as well. The fathers are right; the young people tend to be foolish. The hero must find himself and then comes to accept the woman chosen for him by the parents. The heroine, for all her spunkiness, subordinates her wishes to her father's. The social order is never questioned—neither the supposition that young men of the upper class should marry socially acceptable and wealthy young women nor the notion that a man is admirable if only he resists debauching a woman of the lower class. At worst, then, Goldsmith accepts uncritically some of the hidebound assumptions of his age. At best, however, he expresses a nostalgic longing for order, moderation, and refined simplicity that is never easy to achieve and that may well have been slightly out of date even in his own time. For all its robustness and genial fun, *She Stoops to Conquer* has a mellow nostalgia for the permanent—"old friends, old times, old manners, old books, old wine"—values that, transcending their own age, have retained their universal appeal.

Ironically, it was no easier for Goldsmith to have his second play produced than his first. George Coleman, manager of the Covent Garden theater, who had reluctantly staged *The Good-Natured Man*, again delayed acceptance, in this case until Dr. Samuel Johnson used his influence. There were difficulties with actors, last-minute revisions, quarrels about who should speak the epilogue, and unpleasant rumors that the comedy was "exceedingly Low" and would "certainly be damned."[11] The play finally opened on March 15, 1773, at the very end of the theater season, hardly an auspicious time.

Nonetheless, *She Stoops to Conquer* was an immediate success. On the opening night Goldsmith's famous friends—Dr. Johnson, Sir Joshua Reynolds, Edmund Burke, and the playwright Richard Cumberland—came to encourage applause but found that the audience's spontaneous approval made their efforts unnecessary. At the Author's Benefit on the third night, according to a contemporary reviewer, "The Theatre was filled with the loudest Acclamations that ever rung within its walls."[12] During the first year the play was performed twenty-five times—a large number for the period. Several well-known actors took the principal parts: Edward Shuter played Mr. Hardcastle; John Quick, Tony Lumpkin. Mary Bulkley took the part of Kate and because she was unable to sing, the lyric "Oh marry me" had to be dropped from the script. During the summer of 1773 the enterprising Samuel Foote featured the play at his Haymarket Theater and himself played Tony Lumpkin. Within three months of the opening, there were successful performances in other English towns, in Dublin, and in New York. Before the end of the century, Goldsmith's comedy was put on every few years at all three major London theaters. Quick became famous for his Tony Lumpkin at Covent Garden.

In America *She Stoops to Conquer* was the last important new play given in New York before the Revolutionary War brought about the closing of the theater in 1774. When the New York Company of Comedians went to Charleston and then to Kingston, Jamaica, to a ten-year exile, *She Stoops to Conquer* remained in its repertory. Meanwhile, although the New York theater was officially closed, British officers under the command of Sir Henry Clinton, known as Clinton's Thespians, gave an amateur performance in 1778. After the war, the American Company of Comedians, returned from exile, staged the play every two or three years not only in New York but also in Charleston, Philadelphia, and Boston. In Philadelphia it was featured not as a play but, in deference to the Quakers, as "A Lecture on the Disadvantages of Improper Education Exemplified in the History of Tony Lumpkin"[13] (1779).

During the nineteenth century hardly a year went by without a performance either in London or in one of the English provincial towns. In the early decades of the century John Liston played Tony Lumpkin and Charles Kemble, Marlow. Later, in the 1860s, Miss Herbert, manager of the Saint James Street Theatre in London, was acclaimed for her Kate and Walter Lacy for his Tony. In the 1870s and 1880s, Lionel Brough was called "the best Tony on the stage," and Forbes Robertson alternated in the parts of Marlow and Hastings. In 1881, Lily Langtry made her stage debut as Kate at the Haymarket in London, and in 1883 she toured America in the part.[14]

As for native American performances, the first half of the century saw productions in New York, Philadelphia, St. Louis, and Boston every few years and even a successful tour to the West in 1852 during the Gold Rush.[15] Later, the play became a popular part of the repertory both of the Boston Museum and of Wallack's Theater in New York; Lester Wallack played Marlow for 25 years between 1861 and 1886, and was said to be unrivaled in the part.[16]

The liveliness, bustle, and fun of *She Stoops to Conquer* are caught in this final group scene from the 1949 Old Vic production. At the left, Marlow (Michael Redgrave) is happy with Kate Hardcastle (Diana Churchill), whom he mistook for a barmaid because of her country dress. At the table, center, Squire Hardcastle (Miles Malleson) is still trying to cope with his clownish servants and his mischievous stepson, Tony Lumpkin. Toward the right, Hastings and Constance Neville, the play's secondary lovers, kiss while the frumpish Mrs. Hardcastle looks on disapprovingly. Sets and staging were modeled on the satiric prints of the eighteenth-century artist Rowlandson.
JOHN VICKERS

Of the many twentieth-century English performances, one should single out the Birmingham Repertory Company's of 1927, in which Laurence Olivier took the part of Tony Lumpkin, and Sir Nigel Playfair's London production of 1928, in which Sir Nigel played Tony and Brian Aherne, Marlow. The dangers of too reverent a revival were, however, suggested by the *Times* reviewer, who observed that the play "is homespun in spirit, and Sir Nigel's tendency is to make a fine brocaded satin of it."[17]

The Old Vic, bent on its task of keeping alive great English dramas of the past, staged a number of notable revivals, usually with a memorable cast. In 1932-1933, Peggy Ashcroft played Kate; Roger Livesey, Tony; and Anthony Quayle, the clownish Diggory. In 1939, just before World War II, Ursula Jeans took the part of Kate and John Mills that of Marlow. Then, in 1949, while postwar austerity still prevailed in England, the Old Vic launched a brilliant production with Michael Redgrave as Marlow, Diana Churchill as Kate, and Miles Malleson as Mr. Hardcastle. The sets and staging were modeled on the satiric engravings of Rowlandson. The 1960 Old Vic revival was less noteworthy, except for the decor by Sir Osbert Lancaster.

The last major English production was staged in 1969 when the 69 Theatre Company of Manchester brought its version to London. It was memorable for Tom Courtenay's portrayal of Marlow, complete with a slight stammer and "tongue-tied embarrassment," and for Graham Murray's inventive direction. The hardships of Mrs. Hardcastle's journey, for instance, were made vivid by spotlights sweeping around the theater and by sound effects emanating from various parts of the house.[18]

In the United States the number of productions declined in the early twentieth century. Then The Players chose *She Stoops to Conquer* for their annual revival of a classical play in 1924—Helen Hayes played

Constance Neville—and George C. Tyler presented a successful production with an "all star cast" in 1928.

The most important revival of the play in New York was Maurice Evans's City Center production of 1949. Celeste Holm played Kate; Brian Aherne repeated the part of Marlow he had taken in 1928 in London; and in a piece of inspired casting, Burl Ives was featured as Squire Hardcastle. Brooks Atkinson found Ives "direct and forceful, and portly as well, giving a fine specific gravity to the whole affair," and the play as a whole "affectionately restored."[19] More recently, in 1960, the Phoenix Theater staged a production with Gerry Jedd as Kate and Donald Madden as Marlow that took "a largely farcical approach," with plenty of improvisation, and was described as "full of galloping life."[20]

*She Stoops to Conquer* has had additional life on the stage in countless amateur performances by schools, colleges, and community groups. It has also inspired two operas, one by Sir George Macfarren (1864) and another by Denis Aplvor (1943-1947). It has even been adapted into various musicals, ranging from *The Two Roses* (London, 1904) and *O Marry Me* (New York, 1961) to the lively British rock musical *Liberty Ranch* (London, 1972; Washington, D.C., 1974), in which the action is transposed to the American West. Most recently it was converted into *Chips 'n' Ale* (Louisville, Kentucky, 1974), described as "wild and funny, full of pop-ups and put-downs and incidental rumpus."[21] In this more popular form, too, Goldsmith's comedy seems to retain its vitality.

# The Rivals

Sheridan's first play, *The Rivals* (1775), has enjoyed extraordinary popularity on stage. It is an attractive comedy about young people—about the flirtations, games, ruses, and torments of love—as well as the struggle of the young against the older generation. The play is not without flaws, especially in its surfeit of plot, but Sheridan made up for his lack of experience and control by his remarkable inventiveness and exuberance.

In one of his prologues, Sheridan dedicated his play to the figure of Comedy standing at one side of the stage. He asked why Comedy should be expected to give up her themes of "mirth or love" and why she should be displaced by "The Goddess of the woeful countenance—/The sentimental Muse," whose "votaries weep a flood."[1] Not only did Sheridan clearly prefer laughing to weeping or sentimental comedy, but he explicitly ridiculed some of the sentimental attitudes admired by his contemporaries. Beyond that, however, the play provides a remarkable survey of

illusions, delusions, false expectations as well as conscious deceptions that are timeless in their appeal.

The major source of *The Rivals* was certainly
Sheridan's own recent experiences: his life in the
fashionable resort town of Bath; his attachment to the
charming, capricious Elizabeth Linley; their elopement
prior to their marriage; and his involvement with
rivals, duels, and disapproving fathers.[2] This autobiographical material is, however, shaped by the traditional patterns of comedy: parallel pairs of lovers,
disapproving parent-guardian figures, disguises, and
mistaken identity. Sources for particular scenes have
been found in various eighteenth-century comedies,
notably in Sheridan's mother's unpublished *A Journey
to Bath*.[3] In fact, the play as a whole has a distinctly
"literary" flavor and is saved from conventionality
largely by the countless unexpected twists and turns
of the plot and the odd foibles of some of the characters.

Act I begins with the tantalizing dilemma of the
play's central couple, as revealed in the opening conversation between servants. Captain Jack Absolute is
in love with Lydia Languish, and because she has an
aversion to wealthy, socially acceptable young men,
he has resorted to the ruse of pretending to be an
impoverished ensign named Beverley. Captain Absolute's double identity, involving disguise and deceit, is
bound to lead to complications, particularly as his
father, Sir Anthony Absolute, has just arrived in Bath.

The next scenes, focusing on the women, introduce
further problems. Lydia Languish reveals that her aunt
and guardian Mrs. Malaprop has discovered her love
for Ensign Beverley and has confined her to her rooms.
A sentimental young girl, Lydia indeed seems to be

in love with Beverley chiefly because he is poor and because her aunt disapproves. Her cousin Julia, in turn, has problems with her moody, irrationally jealous fiancé Faulkland. In addition, Mrs. Malaprop has fallen in love with the Irish Sir Lucius O'Trigger and is corresponding with him under the assumed name of Delia. Unknown to anyone, her maid Lucy has led Sir Lucius to believe that he is corresponding with Lydia Languish—a further deception and mistaken identity that adds to the complications.

The last part of Act I brings the first of many un-expected turns of the plot. The strong-minded Sir Anthony Absolute suggests to the equally strong-minded Mrs. Malaprop that his son should marry her niece Lydia. In their first moments on stage, both parent figures are autocratic and opinionated, insisting that Lydia give up her Beverley and unquestioningly accept the young man they have chosen. Mrs. Mala-prop also reveals her particular quirk of misusing words in the most startling fashion. As they talk, it becomes apparent that the conventional plot complications whereby parents or guardians choose marriage partners for their children whom the latter find unacceptable is neatly inverted because the older generation has chosen the very partners the young people want—unbeknown to all concerned.

Act II, focusing on the men, vividly reveals Faulk-land's tormented personality. At first, Faulkland is gloomy and apprehensive about Julia, whom he has not seen in some time. When Jack Absolute and the newly arrived Bob Acres, who has just seen Julia, reassure Faulkland that she is well and indeed in high spirits, he is relieved but then, paradoxically, becomes increasingly depressed, the more he hears about her cheerfulness. A victim of his own imagination, he assumes that Julia is insensitive and uncaring, and so the scene ends as it began, with his perverse, unfounded gloom and jealousy.

Not only is this scene a brilliant character study of Faulkland, but it also plays off the voices of three quite different types against each other. Faulkland's anxious questions are contrasted with Acres' naive replies, and both are contrasted with Jack Absolute's teasing as he alternatingly encourages Acres to give more details about Julia and Faulkland to assume the worst. Absolute is the high-comedy figure here, who knows more than the other two and playfully manipulates them. Acres, on the other hand, is a farcical figure, a dolt from the country in the process of adopting the fashions of the town, whose perceptions are very limited. He adds to the plot complications when he naively reveals that he is in love with Lydia Languish and a rival of Ensign Beverley—quite unaware that Beverley and his old friend Jack Absolute are the same.

In the last big scene of Act II, the focus changes from love to the father-son relationship. Sir Anthony offers to increase Jack's allowance. Jack is delighted until he hears the reason: he is to take a wife. A heated argument ensues in which the father insists that his son must follow orders, whereas the son insists that he loves another woman. Old Absolute works himself up into a blazing rage, all the time emphasizing his patience and mildness. The audience not only laughs at the vivid exhibition of Sir Anthony's irrational, choleric temperament but also enjoys the dramatic irony that comes from knowing, as the combatants do not, that the young woman in question is actually acceptable to both of them.

The second act ends with a slight, unexpected unraveling as Lucy tells Fag, whom she knows only as Ensign Beverley's servant, that Sir Anthony wants his son Captain Absolute to marry Lydia. With this revelation, the plot takes a surprising new turn. For at the beginning of Act III, Jack Absolute already knows that his father will allow him to marry Lydia, and he now plays the part of the repentant, ostentatiously obedient son, willing to propose to any woman his father designates.

This light-hearted central intrigue is interrupted by a more somber scene. The first meeting on stage of Faulkland and Julia dramatizes one of those futile lovers' quarrels experienced by people who perpetually take their emotional temperature. Faulkland accuses Julia of being uncaring, refuses to be reassured, and eventually drives her away in tears. Paradoxically, Faulkland knows that he is being unreasonable but cannot stop himself, and after Julia leaves, he knows that he is in the wrong but blames her. This second brilliant portrayal of Faulkland evokes a double response as the audience sympathizes with Julia but laughs at Faulkland's incorrigible contrariness.

In the middle of Act III the Absolute/Beverley deception comes to the fore when Captain Absolute pays his respects to Mrs. Malaprop as the official suitor of her niece. He immediately hears Mrs. Malaprop's complaint about Lydia's continued interest in Beverley and is even shown a letter of Beverley's that Mrs. Malaprop has intercepted. This letter describes Mrs. Malaprop in the most insulting terms, and dramatic irony is intense as Captain Absolute reads aloud such vivid epithets as "the old weather-beaten she-dragon who guards you"—phrases that we know he himself has penned—while he ostensibly sympathizes with the indignant Mrs. Malaprop.

Next, Jack Absolute meets his Lydia for the first time on stage. She has been summoned by her aunt to meet her suitor Captain Absolute and is overjoyed to meet her Beverley instead. Quick-wittedly, the young man persuades Lydia that he is only masquerading as Captain Absolute. Toward the end of their interview, Mrs. Malaprop listens in and naturally misinterprets their remarks. She assumes that Lydia is rejecting Absolute in favor of her Beverley, whereas Lydia assumes that she is accepting Beverley in the disguise of Absolute. This witty complication leaves both the hero's deception and the heroine's illusions intact.

The tone now changes sharply as Bob Acres and Sir Lucius O'Trigger, an unlikely pair, are brought together in a great scene of farce, and complications mount. Acres, more absurdly foppish than at his first appearance, complains that the woman he loves prefers his rival Beverley. Sir Lucius, inclined to be belligerent, instantly suggests a duel and in a series of blatant *non sequiturs* persuades Acres that "honour" is more important than "right." In fact, Sir Lucius bullies Acres into writing a ludicrous letter of challenge for a duel in King's Mead Fields, where Sir Lucius also has a duel to fight. On stage, the movements of the pugnacious Sir Lucius and the weakening, then falsely euphoric Acres lend themselves to hilarious improvising. And the fun of the scene is intensified by the echoes of Sir Andrew Aguecheek's ridiculous challenge in *Twelfth Night*.

Since it is pure delusion on Acres' part to think that he has a claim on Lydia or a grudge against his rival, really his friend Jack Absolute, and since Sir

Lucius has no reason whatsoever to become involved, the conventional code of honor and the mania for dueling are thoroughly debunked. This debunking is continued in the next scene between Acres and his servant David, with the amusing difference that Acres now takes over Sir Lucius's view of honor, whereas David expresses Acres' own unsteady courage. Nonetheless, the duel is brought one step closer when, ironically, Acres asks Absolute to deliver the challenge to his own other self, Ensign Beverley.

The central scene of Act IV features the expected courtship of Lydia by Captain Absolute, worked out in unexpected ways. Sir Anthony has brought his reluctant son, Mrs. Malaprop her unwilling niece, and both parent figures, in an amusing scene of social embarrassment, urge the young people to play their assigned parts in the wooing. Captain Absolute, finally forced to address Lydia directly, disguises his voice so as not to sound like her Beverley and claims to be overcome by modesty. The scene may well have been influenced by Leontine's forced wooing of Miss Richland in Goldsmith's *The Good-Natured Man*.[4]

Finally, the moment of recognition comes, first to Lydia and then to the others. Captain Absolute, in a tender speech, declares his love for Lydia in his true identity. Sir Anthony is pleased by his son's ingenuity. Even Mrs. Malaprop, although she realizes that young Absolute wrote the insulting letter, is persuaded to forgive him. After these revelations and reconciliations, the expected happy ending seems near.

But this is only Act IV, and so the plot takes another surprising turn. Lydia retains her dislike of conventional arrangements and, far from being pleased by Captain Absolute's proposal, becomes sullen and peevish. In fact, the two engage in a futile lovers' quarrel that parallels Faulkland's and Julia's in Act III. The problem of the young lovers remains as complicated as ever, and ironically, Jack Absolute finds that he is his own worst rival.[5]

The other strands of the plot now reach their greatest complication, while the tone changes rapidly from scene to scene. Farcically, Sir Lucius provokes the astonished Captain Absolute to a duel because the Captain has unwittingly insulted him; the audience is not surprised to find that Absolute is the opponent Sir Lucius mentioned earlier (Act III, sc. 4). In a more serious mood, Faulkland subjects Julia to another test, fabricating the story that a quarrel is forcing him to leave England. In the one purely sentimental scene of the play, full of elevated sentiments and high-flown speeches, Julia staunchly insists on going with Faulkland and so proves her loyalty beyond a doubt. But when Faulkland reveals that he was only testing her, the long-suffering Julia at last turns on him. Bitter about all the pain he has caused her, she flatly rejects him. This climax of the Faulkland-Julia plot ends with Faulkland's cursing his folly and with his realization, finally, that all his problems have been of his own making.

At this point, all the characters move toward King's Mead Fields. In a farcical delaying scene, the servants Fag and David urge the ladies, in tantalizingly long-winded speeches, to hasten to the rescue. Captain Absolute tries to evade his father on the South Parade, pretending implausibly to be "Mr. Saunderson" to conceal his going to the duel.

The actual dueling scene, like all farce, has to be seen on stage to be appreciated. As the oddly assorted belligerents prepare for the fight, the voices of the pugnacious Sir Lucius and the cowardly Acres are again contrasted. The entrance of Captain Absolute and Faulkland brings unexpected confusion when Sir Lucius takes Faulkland for Beverley. This mistaken identity leads Absolute to reveal that he is actually Beverley. Acres has a moment of insight and, being a good sort, refuses to fight his old friend Absolute even though he is his rival. Only Sir Lucius is still spoiling for a fight, and so eventually he and Captain Absolute draw swords. This is the long-expected high point of Act V, the duel that we have been prepared for all along. It pits against each other two surprising opponents—Absolute and the peripheral Sir Lucius, who does not even know that he is also Absolute's rival because he takes his Delia to be Lydia. If this high point is an anticlimax, it well shows the pointlessness of dueling and the hollowness of the code of honor associated with it.

Wisely, the duel is not prolonged. Sir Anthony, arriving on the scene with David and the ladies, quickly puts an end to it. The further unraveling proceeds quickly. Sir Lucius claims his Delia, much to Lydia's surprise, but this mistake moves her finally to accept Captain Absolute. When Sir Lucius persists in regarding Lydia as his correspondent, Mrs. Malaprop comes forward with the astonishing revelation that she is Delia. In an amusing sequence, Sir Lucius thereupon offers Mrs. Malaprop to Captain Absolute, who declines the honor and tries to palm her off on Bob Acres, who in turn also refuses the offer. Instead of the usual matches between minor characters that come about at the end of a comedy, Sir Lucius, Acres, Sir Anthony, and Mrs. Malaprop all remain unattached.

Only the two young couples are united after Julia and Faulkland are, after all, reconciled. The two men then reflect on their similar experiences in tasting "the Bitters, as well as the Sweets of Love" (Act V, sc. 3) and also dwell on the differences between them: Absolute has suffered because of Lydia, whereas Faulkland has brought his suffering on himself. The last lines are the young women's, as Julia looks forward to a more moderate but consequently more lasting kind of happiness than they envisaged earlier. Not only are all the complications successfully resolved, but the young people have also learned something in the process.

The plot of *The Rivals*, appealing in its playful twists and turns, the ingenious bringing together of all the strands at King's Mead Fields, and the extraordinary variety of great comic scenes, also has the drawback of being overly luxuriant. There are loose ends, such as Jack Absolute's suggesting that Mrs. Malaprop help Lydia elope with her Beverley and permit him, as Absolute, to come to the rescue (Act III, sc. 3)— a whole new intrigue that is never developed. Absolute's pretending to be Mr. Saunderson (Act V, sc. 2) and Lydia's and Julia's recapitulations of their experiences (Act IV, sc. 1) are hardly necessary. Such looseness and prolixity remained typical of Sheridan's plays until *The School for Scandal*, in which he finally exerted greater control over an even more complicated plot.

As for the characters, they are traditional comic types and yet extraordinarily rich and varied. Already in this first play Sheridan proved himself a remarkably astute psychologist as well as a masterly comic playwright, able to reveal follies or foibles with ease. The young lovers are more complicated than conventional comedy lovers. And the remaining figures have such distinctive, colorful personalities that, far from being minor characters, they offer the major acting parts.

Lydia Languish is memorable for both her foibles and her complexity. Not only is she the sentimental heroine *par excellence*, with many obvious sentimental traits carried to absurd extremes, but she is also a female Don Quixote, whose head has been turned by too much reading, in this case of sentimental novels (Act I, sc. 2). So bent is she on emotional experiences that she quarrels with her Beverley merely to see how a lover's quarrel feels; she carries her sentimental charity to the poor so far as to refuse her suitor merely because he turns out to be wealthy; and she is determined not to be hemmed in by conventions. Capricious and willful, she is also spirited in a way that belies her last name. Above all, she is charming. She is at her best when, late in the play, she nostalgically recalls her earlier daydreams:

> There had I projected one of the most sentimental elopements!—so becoming a disguise!—so amiable a ladder of Ropes!—Conscious Moon—four horses —Scotch parson—with such surprise to Mrs. Malaprop—and such paragraphs in the Newspapers!—O, I shall die with disappointment.
>
> (ACT V, SC. 1)

Eighteenth-century audiences were no doubt amused by Lydia's theatrical posturing, desire to shock, and general sentimental excesses; modern audiences have found her appealing because her objections to social conventions—to a marriage ceremony, financial settlement, and guardian's consent—prefigure the anti-Establishment attitudes of young people of our own time.

Jack Absolute is the dashing, high-spirited hero, who vastly enjoys his various roles. The fun of his scenes comes from watching him throw himelf into a part—playing the sentimental lover with Lydia, the obedient son with Sir Anthony, the respectful suitor with Mrs. Malaprop—and always extemporizing and embellishing on his ruse. In taking on the disguise of Beverley, Jack Absolute is the type of "double gallant" popular in earlier eighteenth-century comedies and previously explored in Goldsmith's *She Stoops to Conquer*.[6] As in Goldsmith's play, this type is used to ridicule the sentimental hero. But whereas Goldsmith's Marlow is a confused, immature young man with a genuine double identity—he is bashful with ladies of his own class but flirtatious with lower-class girls—Absolute is thoroughly self-possessed and well-integrated, and only pretends to have a second identity—to be poor and sentimental—to fall in with the heroine's illusions. Indeed, in obvious contrast to Lydia, he has a firm sense of reality. He does not despise money or social position and is quite willing to say to Lydia: "Come, come, we must lay aside some of our romance—a little *wealth* and *comfort* may be endur'd after all" (Act IV, sc. 2). He represents the norm or ideal of the play, and his sensible point of view prevails at the end.

Faulkland is a brilliant psychological study of the sentimental type at its most destructive. Utterly egotistic, he anxiously watches the fluctuations of his emotions, and he thinks nothing of tormenting his fiancée by constantly probing her sentiments. In Sheridan's hands, this man of feeling, far from being admirable, as audiences of the 1770s would have expected, appears highly problematic, never at peace with others or himself. Although he is endowed with a remarkably complex neurotic psychology, he is also, however, a distinctly comic figure—as Captain Absolute points out, "a subject more fit for ridicule than compassion" (Act IV, sc. 3). We must remember that Faulkland has only himself to blame and ought to laugh at him accordingly.

Julia, the most conventional of the young lovers, is supposed to represent the ideal of sentiment and good sense. In actual fact, she is so much the passive, long-suffering victim of Faulkland's tormenting that she becomes sentimental in the negative sense, especially when, after the quarrel of Act III, sc. 2, she exits in tears, misunderstood by the man she loves. But in relation to Lydia, she represents the voice of common sense and of social norms, as when she makes clear that she only condoned her cousin's flirtation with Beverley because she knew him to be the eligible Captain Absolute. It is she who has the final words in the play, rejecting excessive passion and settling for a "modest, hurtless" kind of love. In this moderate point of view, she, like Captain Absolute, expresses the norms or standards of the play.[7]

Linked with the main pair of lovers are two magnificent eccentrics, the representatives of the older generation. Broadly conceived and bordering on the farcical, Sir Anthony Absolute and Mrs. Malaprop loom much larger than life whenever they appear on stage.

Sir Anthony is the bullying, hot-tempered father, a type that goes back as far as Roman comedy.[8] But although he is as intransigent as his last name suggests, he is also capable of affection and somehow lovable. Underneath all his bluster he seems to be fond of his son, and he alone of all the men is kind to Mrs.

Malaprop at the end. In this respect, he recalls certain amiable eccentrics in the novels of Sheridan's time: My Father, that opinionated old gentleman in Laurence Sterne's *Tristram Shandy*, or the gruff but benevolent Mathew Bramble in Tobias Smollett's *Humphry Clinker*.

Mrs. Malaprop combines two well-known social-comedy types: the tyrannical guardian and the super-annuated but still man-hunting woman. Her oddest and most distinctive trait, however, is her outrageous misuse of language; her very name suggests her habit of using words that are *mal apropos* or inappropriate in their contexts. Her verbal lapses, funny in themselves, are made even funnier by the obvious pride she takes in them. Not only does Captain Absolute's letter draw attention to her "ridiculous vanity, which makes her dress up her coarse features, and deck her dull chat with hard words which she don't understand," but hearing this criticism read aloud, she rises to the bait and splendidly demonstrates her foible:

> There, Sir!—an attack upon my language! what do you think of that?—an aspersion upon my parts of speech! was ever such a brute! Sure if I reprehend any thing in this world, it is the use of my oracular tongue, and a nice derangement of epitaphs!
>
> (ACT III, SC. 3)

Mrs. Malaprop may be modeled on several literary characters who misuse the language: Shakespeare's Dogberry in *Much Ado About Nothing*, Henry Fielding's Mrs. Slipslop in *Joseph Andrews*, Smollett's Tabitha Bramble in *Humphry Clinker*, and particularly Frances Sheridan's Mrs. Tryfort in *A Journey to Bath*.[9]

But Sheridan certainly outdid his precursors in the verve and extravagance of his character's vocabulary.

The two rivals in the play, Bob Acres and Sir Lucius O'Trigger, are also popular social-comedy types. Even more than Sir Anthony and Mrs. Malaprop, they are broad figures of farce. They, too, are unforgettable oddities, each with a touch of madness of his own.

Bob Acres, one of the best-loved figures of the play, is an inspired combination of several types. The country bumpkin trying to become a town fop, he combines the awkward manners of the country with the ridiculous affectations of the town. In addition, Acres is the blustering fighter, who likes to be called "fighting Bob" (Act IV, sc. 1) but is a coward at heart. In this respect, he recalls not only Shakespeare's Falstaff but also the *miles gloriosus*, the swaggering but chicken-hearted soldier in the comedies of Plautus and Terence.[10]

Sir Lucius O'Trigger is the comic Irishman, true to this stereotype in being a lady's man and a soldier of fortune. Originally much cruder in language and motive, he was disliked by the first-night audience, and in the revised version of the play, his speeches and his interest in marrying for money were toned down.[11] But his fiery temper and pugnacious spirit, proverbially attributed to the Irish, remained, and these make him, even more than Acres, a *miles gloriosus* or swaggering soldier. In fact, this type is ingeniously divided between two characters: Sir Lucius, primarily the swaggerer, and Acres, primarily the coward. The figures of the country booby and the fighting Irishman are brilliantly linked in a memorable "odd couple," reminiscent of

Sir Toby Belch and Sir Andrew Aguecheek in *Twelfth Night* and prefiguring Laurel and Hardy.

All the characters of *The Rivals* are chosen with an eye for balance and contrast, in the best tradition of comedy going back to Plautus and Terence. Everyone is paired: the two parent-guardian figures, the two rivals Sir Lucius and Acres, and, of course, the two sets of lovers. These are particularly well-balanced, for not only is there a contrast between the controlled Jack Absolute and the uncontrolled Faulkland, the whimsical Lydia and the moderate Julia, but each couple also includes one capricious and one sensible partner, with the added variation that the capricious one is the woman in the first pair and the man in the second. For all its seeming ease and casualness, the play has a tight neoclassic sense of form.

Social satire is strong throughout the comedy, reinforcing the satire of the characters' psychological flaws or foibles. Beyond the dominant satire of exaggerated sentimentalism and of the false code of honor leading to foolish duels, the play specifically ridicules the excessive reading of sentimental novels by women, who constituted a new reading public in the eighteenth century, as well as the false, narrow views of women's education held by the older generation.[12] Bob Acres serves to satirize the lack of polish of country squires as well as the ridiculous fashions and manners of the town from hair curlers to French dancing steps (Act III, sc. 4). Even the propensity to maltreat an inferior if one has been maltreated by a superior is ridiculed; the valet Fag, hit by Sir Anthony and abused by Jack Absolute, swiftly turns on an errand boy, introduced for the sole purpose of being kicked and beaten (Act II, sc. 1).

The tone of the play is remarkably varied. Apart from witty satire, it ranges from the sophisticated ironies of the Beverley/Absolute charade to the somberness of the Faulkland-Julia quarrels to the boisterous fun of the Sir Lucius-Acres encounters. All in all, Sheridan has a keen sense of the ridiculous—of odd characters and absurd situations. And although genial humor is not as pervasive as in Goldsmith's *She Stoops to Conquer*, Sheridan's unmistakable fondness for his odder characters with all their foibles provides an engaging touch of tenderness as well.

Quite as varied as the tone is the spirited, inventive style of the comedy. Sheridan, like Goldsmith, was at his best in capturing colloquial speech, as when Jack Absolute, having parodied a sentimental effusion in courting Lydia, undercuts the verbiage with an aside: "If she holds out now the devil is in it!" (Act III, sc. 3). Elsewhere, the colloquialisms are reinforced with vivid, specific details, as when Sir Lucius asks what he should do with Acres' body if he is killed in the duel: "would you chuse to be pickled and sent home?—or would it be the same to you to lie here in the Abbey? —I'm told there is very snug lying in the Abbey" (Act V, sc. 3). Later in the scene, Acres is allowed the satisfaction of quoting these memorable phrases back to the speaker, asking Sir Lucius if he would like to have *his* body pickled after the duel he is insisting on.

It is in Mrs. Malaprop's speeches, however, that Sheridan's flair for language becomes most apparent, particularly his ability to create phrases that are simultaneously ludicrous and evocative. Some of her wording is close to normal in sound, although not in sense—for instance, when she proclaims that a well-educated young woman "should have a supercilious knowledge of accounts;—and as she grew up, I would have her instructed in geometry, that she might know something of the contagious countries. . . ." Other terms are the opposite of what Mrs. Malaprop means, notably, her threat that if the maid Lucy betrays her, "you forfeit my malevolence for ever" (Act I, sc. 2) and her expression of forgiveness: "we will not anticipate the past;—so mind young people—our retrospection will now be all to the future" (Act IV, sc. 2). Best of all are her quasi-poetic images, full of subtle though indefinable overtones: "He is the very Pineapple [pinnacle] of politeness!" she says appreciatively of the flattering Jack Absolute. "It gives me the hydrostatics [hysterics]," she complains at a moment of crisis. And condemning Lydia, she cries out: "She's as headstrong as an allegory [alligator] on the banks of the Nile." Indeed, Mrs. Malaprop brilliantly describes her own language as "a nice derangement of epitaphs" (Act III, sc. 3).

Mrs. Malaprop is not alone in her linguistic oddity. Bob Acres specializes in oaths that change with their context, interjecting "Odds whips and wheels" when talking of travel by coach, "Odd's Blushes and Blooms" when referring to Julia's health (Act II, sc. 1), and "Odds Wrinkles" when offered Mrs. Malaprop at the end (Act V, sc. 3). Mocked here are both the common habit of cursing and the overly literal application of the critical doctrine that "the sound must seem an echo to the sense" (Alexander Pope, *An Essay on Criticism*, Part I, l. 365); Acres insists that an "oath should be an echo to the sense" (Act II, sc. 1).

*The Rivals*, for all its vivid scenes, characters, and dialogue, strikes many theatergoers as a curiously elusive and unfocused play. Yet it is at least loosely unified by some of the great traditional themes of comedy. Certainly, the vagaries of love dominate the proceedings, from the opening scene in which Fag stresses that "LOVE, love" is the cause of the Absolute/Beverley confusion to all the later complications as well as the characters' follies or foibles caused by misconceived, misguided, misplaced, or misunderstood love. Equally pervasive is the theme of illusion and delusion that links Lydia's impractical daydreams and Faulkland's jealous delusions with Acres' and Sir Lucius's illusory code of honor and unfounded hopes of winning Lydia. Sir Anthony and Mrs. Malaprop are deluded about themselves and out of touch with reality as they try to impose their wills on the young people; Mrs. Malaprop's very language is a kind of delusion not properly related to reality. Jack Absolute's pretense of being Beverley is still another illusion, as is Mrs. Malaprop's passing herself off as Delia—these consciously adopted. The ending brings all the characters back to reality as they abjure their extravagant expectations and settle for a moderate happiness.

More generally, the play dramatizes the universal cycle of generations—a traditional theme of comedy that goes back to Plautus and Terence.[13] The young and vigorous Jack Absolute is clearly ready to displace the older generation, Sir Anthony and Mrs. Malaprop, who are ludicrously outmoded in their ideas and richly deserve to be outwitted. In this respect, *The Rivals* tends to be subversive, opposed to convention and the *status quo*. Still, the conflict between the generations is somewhat softened at the end when the young people choose the very partners favored by the older generation, thereby making possible a mellow reconciliation.

With its far-reaching ridicule of many characters, especially those with sentimental leanings, and its emphasis on laughing comedy, the play would seem to be quite as antisentimental as Sheridan proclaimed in his second Prologue. Yet it is not untouched by the cult of sentiment popular in its time. As we have seen, sentiment is indeed valued—provided that it is not excessive or unrealistic and provided that it is held in bounds by good sense. Julia is intended to show this ideal combination, in contrast to the extremes of Lydia and Faulkland. The characterization of Julia, however, also reveals the negative effect of sentimentalism, for her part in the Faulkland scenes is milked for its pathos. On the other hand, it was probably the cult of sentiment that inspired Sheridan to present his eccentric characters with such affection. Perhaps it is this warmth of feeling, along with the extraordinary number of superb acting parts, that has made *The Rivals* such a favorite on the stage.

Yet the play's opening night, on January 17, 1775, was not promising. The performance was an hour too long, neither Edward Shuter as Sir Anthony Absolute nor John Lee as Sir Lucius O'Trigger knew their parts, and Lee could not produce a plausible Irish accent. Still, Henry Woodward as Captain Absolute, Mary Bulkley as Julia, and John Quick as Bob Acres were well received. When the play reopened on January 28, in shortened form and with Lawrence Clinch replacing Lee as Sir Lucius, the reviews were much more favorable.[14]

The comedy was also produced at the Drury Lane in 1777, after Sheridan became manager, and the cast was said to be even better than that at Covent Garden. Reviewers praised Thomas King as Sir Anthony, John

Palmer as Jack Absolute, and Mrs. Abington, "easy and elegant" as Lydia Languish.[15] For the rest of the eighteenth century the play could be seen in both London theaters and in the provinces as well.

Although American theaters were officially closed because of the Revolutionary War, both the British and the new Americans soon put on the play. Clinton's Thespians, British officers serving in New York under Sir Henry Clinton, gave an amateur performance in 1778. The American Company of Comedians, formerly of New York, performed it in Kingston, Jamaica (1780), and later in New York (1786) after their return from exile.[16]

During the nineteenth century *The Rivals* was so popular that it was produced almost annually either in London or in the provinces. In the 1810s and 1820s, Covent Garden had a distinguished cast: Charles Kemble played Jack Absolute; Mr. Liston, Bob Acres; Mrs. Davenport, Mrs. Malaprop; and starting in 1825, the famous Mme. Vestris, Lydia. Charles Kemble also played Faulkland in 1820 at the Drury Lane, whose cast included Mr. Harley as Acres and Mr. Dowton as Sir Anthony. For one night only, in 1817, Dowton played Mrs. Malaprop. Later in the century Mr. and Mrs. Chippendale took the parts of Sir Anthony and Mrs. Malaprop, and Kate Vaughan was a popular Lydia. In 1884, Sir Arthur Wing Pinero collaborated on an "arrangement" of *The Rivals* and took the part of Sir Anthony, while Forbes Robertson played Jack Absolute and Lionel Brough, Acres. Forbes Robertson and Brough continued in those parts for a number of years.[17]

In the United States the play seems to have been performed every few years during the early part of the nineteenth century but reached the height of its popularity only in the second half. From the sixties on, it was in the repertory of two great companies: Lester Wallack's in New York and the Boston Museum. Then, starting in 1880, the much-loved Joseph Jefferson took on the part of Bob Acres, and *The Rivals* became a favorite piece of the Jefferson-Florence Company; W. J. Florence played Sir Lucius and Mrs. John Drew, Mrs. Malaprop. Jefferson, who continued to play Acres for twenty years, condensed the comedy by cutting the part of Julia and greatly reducing that of Faulkland. This version dominated the American stage well into the twentieth century.[18]

Of the many productions given during our own century, only a few can be singled out here. In England, Ben Greet was a well-known Acres from ca. 1899 on; he directed and acted in the Old Vic production of 1916 that also featured Sybil Thorndike as Lydia Languish. Sir Nigel Playfair revived the fuller version of the play in 1925, restoring the Faulkland-Julia quarrel scene; Claude Rains played Faulkland. In the 1938 Old Vic production, Alec Guinness took the part of Acres; however, the London *Times* reviewer was doubtful about the interpretation of Acres as "a gentle loon."[19] A more memorable revival in 1945, immediately after World War II, had "exquisite" designs by Oliver Messel and a commanding performance by Edith Evans as Mrs. Malaprop, who, according to one reviewer, "sweeps all before her" and "presents a mien so fearsome that her disordered speech does indeed seem genuine and not acquired."[20] Nineteen fifty-six saw another major revival, directed by John Clements, who also took the part of Sir Anthony, while Laurence Harvey took that of Jack Absolute. The last

Always delighting in the surprising combination of traditional comic figures, Sheridan in *The Rivals* coupled Sir
Lucius O'Trigger, the fighting Irishman, with Bob Acres,
the awkward country squire bent on becoming a town fop.
In the 1942 Theater Guild production, directed by Eva Le
Gallienne, the greatest modern Acres, Bobby Clark, improvised hilariously while Sir Lucius (Philip Bourneuf)
bullied him into writing a ridiculous letter of challenge to
his unknown rival.

important London production, in 1966, featured Sir
Ralph Richardson as Sir Anthony and, for a time,
Dame Margaret Rutherford as Mrs. Malaprop. These
two great character actors were highly praised, and
Faulkland was recognized as a surprisingly modern,
guilt-ridden type. But the production as a whole seems
to have been disappointing—"strictly non-experimen-
tal," "all fresh and bland and square."[21]

Although the nonexperimental, period-piece approach is typical of many modern productions, a few
English ones have been more enterprising. A 1948
version was done in modern dress. Another, in 1961,
was presented "in the round"; in this, Fay Compton
was greatly praised for her Mrs. Malaprop and
Lawrence Hardy for his Sir Anthony. The 1964
LAMDA production was played on a stark arena stage,
with street lamps and furniture brought in when
needed; here the "modern teen-age rebellion" of Lydia
Languish was emphasized.[22] Finally, John Clements
opened the Chichester Festival Theater Season of 1971
with a new version of *The Rivals*, which he had already
successfully directed in 1956, this time using an open
hexagonal stage. Clements again played Sir Anthony,
and Margaret Leighton, eschewing her usual refined,
ladylike parts, played Mrs. Malaprop, making her less
into a great eccentric than into "a recognizable human
being."[23]

In America the Players Club staged an inventive
revival in New York in 1922, for which Norman Bel
Geddes used "neutral screens" inspired by Stanislavsky
to suggest rather than represent the Bath settings. This
version was repeated in 1923 with a slightly different
cast, including Eva Le Gallienne as Julia. In 1924–1925,
George C. Tyler sponsored an ambitious seventy-week

tour, starring Mrs. Fiske as Mrs. Malaprop; Alexander Woolcott called it a "fantastically triumphant tour, with each town turning out en masse to make the visit jubilant."[24] Mrs. Fiske's appearance in New York in 1930 was, however, far less successful.[25]

The most important American production of this century was undoubtedly the Theater Guild's of 1942, directed by Eva Le Gallienne, who must have remembered her 1923 performance as Julia. Described by Brooks Atkinson "not so much as a comedy of manners as a brawl of manners," this lively version was dominated by Bobby Clark, who improvised hilariously in the part of Bob Acres and was described as a "cyclone of merriment."[26] He was joined by Philip Bourneuf as Sir Lucius and Walter Hampden as Sir Anthony.

There have been numerous other American productions since then—in Chicago (1966), Seattle (1967–68), New Orleans (1967), New Haven (1969—by the Yale Repertory Company, directed by Alvin Epstein) and New York (1975—The Roundabout Theater). There has even been a musical adaptation called *All in Love* (1961) with the script by Bruce Geller and the music by Jacques Urbout. But none of these has come close to the Theater Guild's production, and reviewers of most of these later versions nostalgically recall Bobby Clark's unforgettable portrayal of Bob Acres.

The continued popularity of *The Rivals* is a tribute not only to its literary merits but even more, perhaps, to Sheridan's keen theatrical sense—his superb eye and ear for a striking scene and his ability to create some of the richest acting parts in English comedy.

## St. Patrick's Day

St. *Patrick's Day; or, The Scheming Lieutenant* (1775) is a short, breezy farce. A mere sketch, it was intended as an "afterpiece" to follow the main play of the evening.

Farce is a popular English genre, often presented as an afterpiece from the late seventeenth century on. It concentrates on very funny situations, usually involving slapstick, tricks, and even acrobatics. Farces may or may not have coherent intrigues to hold together the various scenes. And they are content with flat, exaggerated type characters. Some of the eighteenth-century farces are shockingly crude, but others, including Sheridan's, are amusingly fanciful. Because no attempt is made to stay within the bounds of plausibility, the fun comes from watching the inventiveness of the playwright as he creates his absurdly exaggerated characters and situations as well as the ingenuity of the actors as they embroider on the material. Still more than other dramatic works, farces can best be judged when seen on stage: so much depends on the acting, stage business, and even extemporaneous additions during the actual performance.

*St. Patrick's Day* is loosely held together by a slight romantic intrigue: the ingenious Irish lieutenant's wooing of Lauretta in spite of her parents' violent opposition. The main emphasis is not, however, on the love relationship but on Lieutenant O'Connor's ruses to outwit Lauretta's narrow-minded father, Justice Credulous. Intertwined with this intrigue are the exploits of the soldiers stationed in the small provincial town—their attempts to find recruits and to help their lieutenant win his girl. The play is entitled *St. Patrick's Day* not only because it is set on that particular day but also because it honors the Irish, whose wit and ingenuity win in the end.

Sheridan was probably influenced by his father Thomas Sheridan's farce *The Brave Irishman; or, Captain O'Blunder* (1743), still occasionally performed in Dublin and London in the early 1770s.[1] It featured a comic Irishman, the butt of many practical jokes, who unexpectedly turns out to be more good-natured than the other men and who wins the heroine. Sheridan's recruiting scenes may have been inspired by George Farquhar's *The Recruiting Officer* (1706).

The main attractions of Sheridan's farce are the two ruses of Lieutenant O'Connor, both involving extravagant disguises. First, with the help of Dr. Rosy, O'Connor masquerades as "Honest Humphry," a country yokel whom Justice Credulous employs to protect his daughter from the much-feared Lieutenant O'Connor. Dramatic irony is intense as the clever lieutenant plays the ignorant oaf and Justice Credulous, proud of having at last foiled the lieutenant, remains oblivious of the fact that he has himself introduced the snake into his garden. The lieutenant continues to deceive Justice Credulous by letting him overhear a prearranged temptation: several of O'Connor's soldiers offer "Honest Humphry" a bribe, which he indignantly refuses. Eventually, O'Connor and his Lauretta meet. She first scorns him as a country booby, then recognizes him, and they embrace just as the justice returns. The young people improvise a story about Lauretta's dizzy spells, but Credulous is not so credulous as all that, and at the high point of the scene, he pulls off the young man's disguise (Act II, sc. 2).

This setback leads to the second ruse and disguise. Justice Credulous receives a letter in which the lieutenant claims to have poisoned the justice's morning chocolate. The justice becomes an instant hypochondriac, and Dr. Rosy, again helping the lieutenant, confirms that many dangerous symptoms are becoming visible. The lieutenant now enters, in the outlandish guise of a German quack who is supposed to be expert in curing poisonings. In fake Latin, with English word roots still audible, the quack first diagnoses the illness, then demands a great deal of money for a cure, and finally offers a free cure in exchange for the hand of Lauretta. Justice Credulous accepts the last offer only because he is sure that his daughter will never consent. While he writes out his agreement, the quack writes the prescription for his miraculous cure. The expected moment of revelation comes when the lieutenant throws off his disguise and the justice reads that his cure is at hand in the shape of "your affectionate Son in law, O'Connor" (Act II, sc. 3). After a few more angry demurrals, Credulous and his wife Bridget give their consent, and all go off to celebrate the wedding.

The characters of this little bagatelle are sharply

drawn types. The most memorable is Lieutenant O'Connor, the dashing hero, who is quick-witted, inventive, and adept at playing unlikely roles. O'Connor's most distinctive trait, however, is that he is Irish, with all this implied in the eighteenth century: a lively, buoyant personality, on the one hand, but a social outsider on the other. English comedies often ridiculed Irishmen, and so it must have pleased Sheridan, Irish himself, to convert this type into the debonair hero of his piece.

The play's second vivid character is the doctor, called Dosy in contemporary reviews but Rosy in the printed text. O'Connor's benevolent helper, he is gently mocked as a man of sentiment, full of excessive nostalgia for his dead wife and given to Christian-Stoic reflections at inopportune moments. He also has a verbal oddity, a special vocabulary of medical metaphors. When he reminisces about his wife—"Ah! poor Dolly! . . . such an arm for a Bandage—Veins that seem'd to invite the Lancet—. . . Her Mouth round, and not larger than the mouth of a penny Phial!" (Act I, sc. 1)—he gives a delightful medical version of the Petrarchan lover's catalogue of his mistress's best features.

The remaining characters are more one-dimensional. Lauretta, the lieutenant's attractive prize, is willful and sentimental but comes to life only in an early scene in which she contradicts her mother and expresses a young girl's absurd daydreams: ". . . Give me the bold, upright, noble Youth," she exclaims, "—who makes love one day, and has his head shot off the next" (Act I, sc. 2). Her mother Bridget is wholly a stock type, the conventional mother dissuading her daughter from an unsuitable marriage and later the avaricious wife whose only fear is that her husband will spend too much money before he dies. As for Justice Credulous, he is as gullible as his name suggests and is furthermore the choleric father, whose roots lie in the irascible old men of Roman comedy. The soldiers and recruits, finally, remain anonymous and are identified only by rank, occupation, or nationality.

The play includes some blunt but amusing social satire. Through Justice Credulous, the legal profession is made to seem totally ineffectual. Through Dr. Rosy and the lieutenant in his guise of German quack, the medical profession appears as sheer charlatanism. The army is ridiculed for its recruiting practices—both the crude enticements offered and the ignorant type of men who enlist. The outrageous behavior of the soldiers quartered in a small town is also satirized. The perpetual antagonism between the soldiers and the townsmen is, in fact, one of the key motivating factors in the play, for Justice Credulous is categorically opposed to his daughter's marrying an army man.

The social satire as well as the portrayal of family relationships reveal a sharply antiauthoritarian and anti-Establishment point of view. Throughout, the play mocks the staid behavior of the representatives of society, Justice and Mrs. Credulous, and gives a sympathetic view of the younger generation. Above all, the outsider who undermines authority is glamorized in Lieutenant O'Connor—the Irishman who outwits the English Establishment and the dashing soldier who outmaneuvers mere civilians. At the end, when Justice Credulous tells O'Connor: "Forswear your Country, and quit the Army—and I'll receive you as my Son in law," the lieutenant staunchly refuses to disown either Ireland or his career, and it is this show of spirit that makes him deserve to win his girl.

Sheridan wrote *St. Patrick's Day* as a vehicle for the needy actor Lawrence Clinch, who had made a success of Sir Lucius O'Trigger in *The Rivals*. The farce opened on May 2, 1775, and was performed at Covent Garden thirteen more times during its first year. Clinch played O'Connor, while John Quick, famous for his Tony Lumpkin, and Bob Acres, played Dr. Rosy. The play remained in the repertory of Covent Garden even after Sheridan became manager of the Drury Lane, and during the next few years it was also performed in Bath, Liverpool, Bristol, and Ireland.[2]

The few surviving programs reveal that the play was produced occasionally in the early nineteenth century: in Liverpool (1801), Chester (1811), London (1816 and 1831), and Newcastle (1820). The last known twentieth-century production dates back to 1917, when Ben Greet staged it, together with *The Critic*, during his "Sheridan Week" at the Royal Victoria Hall.[3] Although *St. Patrick's Day* is a very minor piece and will hardly be revived in our time, it is not without charm and verve.

## The Duenna

With *The Duenna* (1775), written a few months after *St. Patrick's Day*, Sheridan turned to a genre related to his two earlier comedies but with other possibilities as well: the comic opera. To the romantic intrigue, farce, and satire that were already his forte, he added tender or humorous songs. *The Duenna* was a huge success in its own time but has not retained its popularity. Modern audiences are likely to find it frivolous, often implausible, and at times objectionable in playing on the audience's anti-Semitic and anti-Catholic prejudices. On the other hand, it is also lively and melodious.

Set in Spain, the opera deals with several pairs of lovers and particularly with a duenna or chaperone who, instead of guarding her young charge, actually helps her to elope and marry the man she loves. Meanwhile, the duenna masquerades as the young girl and wins the girl's undesirable suitor, a ridiculous older man, for herself.

Sheridan probably became interested in this story because of his own experiences with his wife Elizabeth, who, as a young girl, had been pursued by a much older man and with whom Sheridan had eloped before their marriage.[1] He also quite possibly drew on his mother's tale *Eugenia and Adelaide*, which featured a duenna and a convent along with the conventional double lovers.[2]

The music was partly composed for the opera and partly adapted from existing melodies. Sheridan's father-in-law and brother-in-law, Thomas Linley senior and junior, were in charge of the music, but they were hampered by not seeing the full libretto, which Sheridan was still devising in London while they were working in Bath. The younger Linley is now known to have created most of the newly composed songs.[3] But the correspondence shows that Sheridan commissioned the music and shaped the whole. Always eager for variety, he consciously combined polite love lyrics with farcical arias and with the familiar folksongs of the ballad opera popular in England since John Gay's *The Beggar's Opera* (1726).

The plot of *The Duenna*, juggling the exploits of two pairs of young and one pair of older lovers, is intricate and unashamedly contrived. Donna Louisa is in love with the impoverished Don Antonio, but her father Don Jerome insists on her marrying the rich old Isaac Mendoza, variously described as a Portuguese and a Jew. At the same time, Donna Clara is being wooed by Louisa's brother Don Ferdinand, but her parents are forcing her to enter a convent. To complicate matters, Ferdinand is jealous of Antonio, who was once in love with Clara.

It is the songs that enliven the explanations in the first scenes. The opening features a charming *aubade*, a song greeting the dawn, with which Antonio and

Louisa communicate their love to each other until they are interrupted by old Jerome's irritable complaint, also in song, about being disturbed in his sleep. The four love lyrics of scene 2 reveal Ferdinand's and Antonio's contrasting attitudes, ranging from blind infatuation and jealousy to cool appraisal of the loved one. These lyrics follow each other in short order and, like most of the subsequent songs, reinforce the spoken dialogue.

With scene 3, the main comic complications begin. Louisa's duenna Margaret, who wants to catch Isaac Mendoza for herself, brings about her dismissal but then remains in the house. The veiled figure who departs, as the audience realizes, is Louisa, in search of her Antonio. A brief meeting between Louisa and Clara in the piazza shows that both girls have left home. Complications mount when Louisa meets Isaac for the first time but pretends to be Clara, and Isaac sends her off to Antonio so as to divert his attention from Louisa. Ironically, Isaac is, of course, sending the very Louisa he wishes to marry into the arms of his rival.

From his entrance in Act I, scene 4, Isaac is set up as a dupe heading for a fall. First seen admiring himself in a pocket mirror, he is puffed up with vanity and proud of his cunning. This scene is a prelude to the farcical scene in Act II, one of the high points of the opera, in which Isaac unwittingly woos the wrong woman, the duenna Margaret, whom he takes for Louisa.

The courtship scene is full of absurd incongruities. Margaret coyly sings "When a tender maid/Is first essayed"—a lyric far from appropriate to her age and looks. Isaac cannot suppress his surprise at her age and beard, and she is equally blunt about his appearance.

Eventually, Isaac blurts out a proposal. Margaret, to maintain her ruse, insists on an elopement, and Isaac agrees, cunningly thinking he can avoid a marriage settlement. He does not question the identity of his bride even when his friend Carlos enters and is taken aback by her ugliness. The scene ends with Carlos's melodious "Ah! sure a pair was never seen,/So justly form'd to meet in nature"—effusive praise that stands in ironic contrast to the actual appearance of the couple.

Blatant coincidence increases the complications in Act III. No sooner does Don Jerome receive a letter from Isaac announcing his elopement with Louisa (actually Margaret) than he receives a second letter from the real Louisa, who has meanwhile joined her Antonio and who writes in such ambiguous terms that she appears to be ready to marry Isaac. Jerome writes his consent to the marriage and orders a celebration for that very night.

Complications—the result of disguise and mistaken identity—now multiply, and the action becomes still more contrived. Ferdinand's jealousy reaches absurd extremes. In Act III, sc. 3, set in the convent where Clara is staying, Ferdinand assumes that the girl walking off with Antonio is Clara (it is actually Louisa) and ignores the veiled nun in front of him (actually Clara). At least, however, his jealousy convinces Clara of Ferdinand's love.

These romantic complications are interrupted by another scene of farce, this one quite extraneous to the plot. A group of hypocritical monks guzzle wine and sing a raucous song while pretending to be at prayer. One of them, Brother Paul, agrees to perform a clandestine marriage only after he is bribed. But just as he is about to marry Louisa and Antonio, he is stopped by the still deluded Ferdinand.

The unraveling proceeds quickly. In the course of a lively duet, "Turn thee round I pray thee," two veiled young women pull Ferdinand from side to side until, at the moment of revelation, both drop their veils and Ferdinand recognizes his sister Louisa, on the one hand, and his beloved Clara, on the other. The scene's concluding chorus, "Oft' does Hymen smile to hear," augurs well for both young couples.

The unraveling of Isaac's misconceptions comes last. This long-awaited recognition scene, set in Don Jerome's "Grand Saloon," is once more broad farce. When Isaac brings in his bride, Jerome forgivingly opens his arms to his daughter Louisa only to realize, with a start, that he is faced with the duenna instead. The ironic moment is extended as the duenna continues to pretend to be his daughter and Isaac urges his "charmer" to throw her "snowy arms" about her father's neck even after Jerome has recognized "old Margaret."

But when the real Louisa and Antonio arrive, the truth is finally revealed. All agree that Isaac has over-reached himself in trying to marry Louisa without a settlement and that he deserves the spouse he has got. When Isaac once more mentions the duenna's age and ugliness, she is allowed her turn at insulting him: "Dares such a thing as you pretend to talk of beauty— . . . a pair of eyes like two dead beatles in a wad of brown dough. A beard like an artichoke, with shrivell'd jaws that wou'd disgrace the mummy of a monkey." With these animal and vegetable images, Isaac is thoroughly deflated. At last view, he is threatening to flee to the ends of the earth and

Margaret is threatening to pursue him. Thereupon the problems of the young people are quickly resolved. Both couples reveal that they are already married and win Don Jerome's approval. With the entrance of a chorus of masqueraders, the opera ends in song, dance, and general celebration.

The complicated plot is managed with considerable skill, especially the intertwining of the three intrigues that is achieved by having Louisa masquerade as the duenna in Act I and as Clara in Acts II and III, while the duenna masquerades as Louisa throughout. The resulting misunderstandings embroil all the major characters, particularly Isaac and Don Jerome, until the unraveling of Act III sets everything to rights. Yet there is also some extraneous material. Don Carlos, really just a double of Isaac, seems to have been introduced chiefly because of the performer's vocal powers. The Spanish dance at the end of Act II and the guzzling monks of Act III are not essential, although they add variety to the whole.

As for the characters, most of them are simple types, appropriate for an opera that has musical as well as plot complications. The young people represent four obvious kinds of lovers: Louisa is lively and enterprising; Clara, melancholy and retiring; Ferdinand, jealous and often frustrated; Antonio, witty and successful. Don Jerome is the tyrannical father *par excellence*, and the duenna Margaret combines the familiar comic types of resourceful servant and older husband-hunting woman.

Yet some of the characters are also endowed with surprising touches. Clara, for instance, is amusingly ambivalent about her feelings. In her plaintive song

"When sable night, each drooping plant restoring" she is worried not about her suitor's importunity but about her own willingness to give herself, and when she warns Louisa to keep her whereabouts secret, she gives explicit directions for how Ferdinand can find her (Act I, sc. 5). Don Jerome has an unexpected *joie de vivre* that comes out in his drinking songs. And Margaret is given a surprising extra farcical touch through her frequently mentioned beard.

Isaac, the play's most vivid character, is also a combination of familiar types. Most obviously, he is the stage Jew, analogous to the Irishman, Frenchman, and other national types often ridiculed in eighteenth-century comedies. The anti-Semitic stereotyping rampant in Sheridan's day accounts for Isaac's small stature and beard as well as for his brashness and habit of self-congratulation.[4] With ironic innuendo, Isaac is not even allowed to be a bona fide Jew but is a recent convert to Christianity, likened to the blank pages between the Old and New Testament (Act I, sc. 3).

In addition, Isaac is the older man bent on acquiring a young wife, the proverbial December in pursuit of May. But above all, he is a braggart, proud of his Machiavellian cunning, who offers the amusing spectacle of the "overreacher" who is undercut, or "a knave become the dupe of his own art" (Act III, sc. 7). Yet even Isaac is, for a moment, humanized when he suddenly shows a fear of beautiful young girls, and this fear, expressed in his song "Give Isaac the nymph who no beauty can boast" (Act II, sc. 2), takes some of the sting out of his being trapped by plain old Margaret. Nonetheless, he remains a broadly farcical figure, strong enough to hold the center of the stage.

Both the dialogue and the songs are lively and inventive. What makes the style of *The Duenna* especially memorable is the intrusion of startlingly blunt colloquialisms in the midst of elegant speeches or songs. In the opening scene, for instance, the lyrical tenderness of Antonio and Louisa is sharply undercut by the prosaic irritation of Don Jerome. The quatrains of the young people, sung allegro, are followed by the father's staccato

> What vagabonds are these I hear
> Fid[d]ling, fluting, rhyming, ranting,
> Piping, scraping, whining, canting,
> Fly, scurvy minstrels, fly.

The choice of words associated with unpleasant noises and the use of dactyls, unusual in English lyrics, make this a rude and funny interruption of what the lovers imagine to be beautiful music. The moods continue to alternate in the following trio, in which the lovers bid each other fond farewell while the father callously threatens to use his shotgun:

> LOUISA: ⎫ We soon perhaps, may meet again
> ANT: ⎬ For tho' hard fortune is our foe,
>     ⎭ The god of love will fight for us.
> JER: Reach me the Blunderbuss.
> ANT: & LOU: The god of love, who knows our pain.
> JER: Hence, or these slugs are thro' your brain.
> (ACT I, SC. I)

Similar intrusions of the colloquial are part of the fun of the Isaac-duenna wooing scene of Act II. After some high-flown dialogue, the duenna declares:

". . . When I saw you, I was never more struck in my life." "That was just my case too, madam; I was struck all of a heap for my part," Isaac replies with an honesty lost on the duenna but not on the audience. A little later Isaac, in an aside, tells his friend Carlos of his successful courtship:

> CARLOS: Where is your mistress?
> ISAAC: There, you booby, there she stands.
> CARLOS: Why she's dam'd ugly.
> ISAAC: Hush! (*Stops his mouth*)
> DUENNA: What is your friend saying, Signor?
> ISAAC: O ma'am, he is expressing his raptures at such charms as he never saw before, hey Carlos?
> CARLOS: Aye, such as I never saw before, indeed.
> (ACT II, SC. 2)

These brash comments, expressed in very direct colloquial speech, are amusingly incongruous in the never-never world of romantic comic opera.

The musical settings for the songs support but do not obscure the texts. Usually they echo the moods, both in the love lyrics and in the drinking songs. In the monks' "This bottle's the sun of our Table" (Act III, sc. 5), the rollicking tune ironically emphasizes the worldliness of the singers. Occasionally, musical punning of the sort made famous by George Frederick Handel is introduced. For instance, when Clara renounces the convent in "Adieu thou dreary pile" (Act III, sc. 4), the phrase "sullen echo" is accompanied by an echo passage on the oboe, and "I fly" is expressed in an extended coloratura flight. But on the whole, the music is remarkably subdued and calls little attention to itself.

The lightheartedness of the libretto and the pleasantness of the music do not prevent *The Duenna* from having some satiric bite. Suitors intent on marrying for money, unlovely people who think themselves lovable, and tyrannical fathers beset by disobedient daughters or servants are ridiculed throughout. Authoritarianism is attacked within the family and also in the larger institution of the Church—the worldly, hypocritical monks are unworthy of the authority that they represent.[5] Some of the extravagancies of romantic love are also exposed. However, as in *The Rivals* and *St. Patrick's Day*, the older people are mocked more broadly than are the young, and it is the young who eventually have their way. Like Sheridan's earlier plays, *The Duenna* is an irreverent, slightly subversive, anti-Establishment piece of fooling.

The comic opera was first performed at Covent Garden on November 2, 1775, with John Quick, famous for his Tony Lumpkin in *She Stoops to Conquer* and Bob Acres in *The Rivals*, taking the part of Isaac. Don Carlos was played by Michael Leoni, who had a fine lyrical voice but was almost incomprehensible in speech, and so Carlos's spoken lines were kept to a minimum. *The Duenna* was an extraordinary success; 75 performances were recorded for 1775–1776. Pirated versions were staged in Dublin in 1777, one of them with the new title *The Governess*, and these were later occasionally used in London as well.[6] The piece was produced in Kingston, Jamaica, starting in 1779 by the American Company of Comedians exiled from New York by the American Revolution. On their return to the mainland, they presented it in 1787 not only in New York but also in Philadelphia and Baltimore. An adaptation called *The Elopement* was given in Charleston in 1786.[7]

The high point of *The Duenna*, Sheridan's comic opera that alternates romantic intrigue with farce, comes when the ugly old Isaac Mendoza courts the equally ugly old duenna Margaret under the mistaken impression that she is the marriageable young Louisa. In the 1954 London production, Isaac (Gerald Cross) was understandably puzzled by the age, appearance, and determination of the lady he was wooing.

ANGUS MCBEAN PHOTOGRAPH, HARVARD THEATRE COLLECTION

*The Duenna* remained popular for many years. William Hazlitt considered it "a perfect work of art," endowed with "the utmost sweetness and point."[8] It was displaced from the repertory only in the mid-nineteenth century when Italian opera came into vogue. By the twentieth century the full musical score was lost, and yet some interest in the piece remained. Nigel Playfair put on a revival at the Lyric, Hammersmith, in 1924. Another production was staged in 1954, with Gerald Cross as Isaac, Joan Plowright as Clara, and new music by Julian Slade. Still another was mounted at the University of Western Australia in 1963.[9]

In addition, *The Duenna* has twice been adapted into a new opera. Sergei Prokofiev became aware of Sheridan's text in 1940, in the midst of World War II, and is said to have exclaimed: "But this is champagne! One can make an opera out of this in the style of Mozart, Rossini."[10] He not only composed the music but also collaborated on the libretto of his version, entitled *Betrothal in a Monastery* (1941). Although he kept the outlines of Sheridan's plot, he transformed Isaac Mendoza into a rich fish merchant. The Russian text was retranslated into English by Jean Karsavina, and this version was given fifty-three performances by the Lemonade Opera of New York during the summer of 1948. Also in the early 1940s, the Anglo-Spanish composer Roberto Gerhard set Sheridan's text to music that has been described as a blend of "Spanishry with neoclassic and serial technique."[11]

In 1976, finally, efforts were made to restore as much of the original score as possible and to stage a full-scale revival. Under the scholarly direction of Dr. Roger Fiske, the Opera da Camera of London gave several spirited performances. The London *Times* reviewer gave a measured appraisal that probably does justice to the work as a whole, finding it "a harmlessly undemanding and amusing concoction," whose musical numbers, although charming, are less memorable than Sheridan's "barbed and witty text."[12]

# The School for Scandal

A dazzling social comedy, *The School for Scandal* is famous for its great scenes and brilliant dialogue. Not only is Sheridan said to have "crowned his reputation" with it, but it has also been called the high point of laughing comedy in the eighteenth century.[1]

*The School for Scandal* was indeed written when Sheridan was at the height of his power. The play shows remarkable control over an intricate plot that traces parallel intrigues involving two brothers with contrasting styles of life and differing romantic attachments, an incongruously matched married couple, and assorted gossipmongers who maliciously comment on all concerned. The scope is broader than in Sheridan's earlier plays, for social as well as personal relationships are included and vices as well as follies and foibles are ridiculed. Sophisticated, witty scenes predominate, but the boisterous fun of farce is not excluded. And the whole is unified by the universal comic theme that always fascinated Sheridan: the discrepancy between surfaces and substance, appearance and reality, delusion and truth.

The comedy may have been inspired partly by Sheridan's own experiences. Possibly the two contrasting brothers are modeled on Sheridan himself and his more staid and prudent brother, whom he did not entirely admire, and conceivably even on two sides he recognized in his own personality. The stings of gossip he had experienced at first hand after his elopement with Elizabeth Linley and the subsequent duels in London and Bath. Perhaps Elizabeth's earlier notorious involvement with a much older man suggested the pairing of the young Lady Teazle with the older Sir Peter Teazle[2] as well as reinforced Sheridan's aversion to scandalmongering. These autobiographical elements are, however, mere seeds that are transformed into a more universal, quite impersonal whole. A number of scenes are, furthermore, suggested by earlier social comedies.

The plot of *The School for Scandal* may appear contrived, especially when presented in summary. But in the theater, it is fascinating to watch the heaping of complications that reveal the characters' flaws, the spinning of diverse threads that come together in one climactic scene, and the eventual untangling of the whole knotty web.

True to its title, the play opens with a scene of scandalmongering. The chatter of two figures with the destructive names of Lady Sneerwell and Snake introduces the Surface brothers, the older one, respected and "amiable"; the younger, wild and dissipated. The first, Joseph, seems attached to Lady Sneerwell, while the second, Charles, is fond of Maria. Sir Peter Teazle is guardian of the Surface brothers and of Maria, his niece. The audience's expectations are immediately reversed, however, when Lady Sneerwell explains that Joseph is interested not in her but in Maria or at least in her money, and that she, Lady Sneerwell, is interested not in Joseph but in his brother Charles. She is, in fact, trying to discredit Charles in Maria's eyes by circulating scandalous falsehoods about him. The expectations about Joseph Surface are also quickly reversed, for, according to Lady Sneerwell, although he is known as a "man of sentiment," he is really "artful, selfish and malicious"—a hypocrite who hides behind a cloak of the sentimentalism so much in vogue at the time. From the start, appearances and reality differ sharply in this society of the town.

A series of striking solo or duo entrances brings the other town figures on stage. Joseph arrives first and immediately confirms Lady Sneerwell's view of him. Reporting on his brother's increasing financial difficulties, he uses noble-sounding phrases of benevolence and charity typical of the man of sentiment until Lady Sneerwell tells him to stop moralizing—he is among friends.

Next to enter is Maria, the first of the good characters. She just has time to express her detestation of gossiping before Mrs. Candour, one of the chief scandalmongers, sweeps in, soon followed by Sir Benjamin Backbite and his uncle Crabtree. The three give a dazzling display of the art and malice of gossiping, incidentally providing the news that Charles Surface is in such financial distress that all his possessions have been sold except for a few family pictures.

Scene 2 of Act I introduces a second plot strand involving the Teazles. Sir Peter's soliloquy reveals that he has just saddled himself with a wife much younger than he. Although he chose a modest country girl, she has taken on the worst habits of the town, and they have been quarreling ever since their marriage. In a brief exchange with the steward Rowley, the grumbling Sir Peter claims that "the Fault is entirely hers . . . I am the sweetest Temper'd Man alive"—suggesting a considerable lack of self-knowledge.

Sir Peter's blindness also extends to the Surfaces. Wishing his niece Maria to marry Joseph rather than Charles, Sir Peter praises Joseph as "a man of sentiment" and damns Charles for frittering away his inheritance. In contrast, the seemingly trustworthy Rowley dislikes Joseph and attributes Charles's problems merely to the wildness of youth. At this point, the crucial plot complication is introduced with the news that Sir Oliver, the rich uncle of the Surfaces and an old friend of Sir Peter's, has just arrived from the East Indies. He wants his return kept secret so as to test the character of his nephews. So the truth about the two young men is bound to come out in spite of all appearances.

Act II, scene 1, shows the Teazles in action and vividly displays their foibles: they cannot help irritating each other but seem to thrive on their bickering. Lady Teazle refuses to acknowledge her husband's authority and defends her extravagances as a necessary part of town life, while Sir Peter annoys her by recalling her simple country background. The next scene, in Lady Sneerwell's drawing room, shows the Teazles in society. Lady Teazle seems to have learned much since coming to town, for she outdoes Mrs. Candour and Sir Benjamin Backbite in malicious comments. Furthermore, she has acquired a taste for flirtation and, to complicate the plot, has her eye on Joseph.

In fact, the love intrigue now thickens, as Joseph tries to woo Maria but is interrupted by the visibly jealous Lady Teazle. Yet it appears that Lady Teazle wants Joseph "as a Lover no further than Fashion requires." Theirs is an ambiguous relationship, at this point a matter of mere appearances and as superficial as many other relationships in the play.

The last scene of Act II and the first of Act III set in motion the expected tests of the Surface brothers. Sir Oliver arrives and shows himself more perceptive than Sir Peter by distrusting Joseph in spite of his noble sentiments and by not being disturbed by reports of Charles's wildness. Sir Oliver decides to pretend to be a poor relation, Mr. Stanley, and ask the two brothers for aid. Because charity is the accepted sign of a good heart in the sentimental tradition, this is a very appropriate trial of the young men's benevolence. But then the moneylender Moses arrives, and Sir Oliver decides to play Moses' friend Mr. Premium, another moneylender, to test Charles. In short, Sir Oliver will disguise himself as Mr. Stanley to test Joseph's benevolence and as Mr. Premium to test Charles's prudence, thereby testing the crucial character trait of each young man.

These scenes of disguise, deception, and mistaken identity are, however, delayed by another Teazle scene. In one of the most memorable comic scenes of the play, they quarrel again. This time, ironically, they try to be agreeable but almost at once squabble about which of them ordinarily begins their squabbles. The quarrel continues until Sir Peter loses his temper to the point of threatening a separation or divorce. Besides vividly demonstrating the foibles of Sir Peter and Lady Teazle, this so-called "tiff-scene" also motivates

Lady Teazle's later behavior by dramatizing the lack of harmony in her marriage.

Only after this domestic interlude does Charles Surface appear for the first time. Contrary to expectations, the impression he makes in Act III, sc. 2, is very bad. When "Mr. Premium" and Moses arrive, Charles is carousing boisterously with his friends and raucously singing "Here's to the maiden of bashful fifteen." The young men insult and patronize Charles's potential creditors. The dramatic irony of having Charles behave like a libertine and wastrel in front of the very uncle he ought to impress reaches its peak when Charles declares himself willing to sell his last remaining possessions, the family portraits. Sir Oliver pretends to laugh at the joke of selling one's ancestors but actually concludes that Charles is an utter spendthrift. "Oh, the prodigal!" are Sir Oliver's last words as he leaves the stage, and so Act III ends with an emphasis on misleading appearances.

Act IV, scene 1, presents the actual auctioning of the portraits, the famous "picture scene." The portraits are no mere stage props but become symbolic of the staid Surface clan. Charles behaves outrageously as he produces his grandfather's chair to serve as auctioneer's "pulpit" or block, and a parchment roll inscribed with the family tree to serve as hammer, and then lets his worthy ancestors be knocked off for very little money. In this boisterous scene of farce, Charles appears totally callous.

But this low point is followed by a surprising reversal. Charles refuses to sell the last remaining portrait, a painting of Sir Oliver. Dramatic irony is again strong as Charles resists Mr. Premium's urging, unaware that he is Sir Oliver. Charles's reason is simple but significant: "The Old Fellow has been good to me" (Act IV, sc. 1). With this spontaneous gratitude, Charles reveals that he has a good heart after all. In return, Sir Oliver instantly changes his view of Charles and now considers him no longer a profligate but "A Dear extravagant Rogue!" And in the next scene, when he hears that Charles is sending some of the money he has just acquired to the unfortunate Stanley, Sir Oliver decides to pay off Charles's debts. We are to assume that Charles's charity, the sign of his good heart, makes him worthy of this rescue.

Before Sir Oliver proceeds to test Joseph, the focus returns to the Joseph-Lady Teazle intrigue. The scene that follows, set in Joseph's library, is one of the most famous in English comedy, dazzling for its surprises, reversals, and great theatrical moments. It begins with Joseph's calculated attempt to seduce Lady Teazle. Hypocritically, he sympathizes when she complains that her name has been falsely linked with Charles Surface, and with brilliant casuistic arguments he suggests that if her husband does not trust her, she might as well give him grounds for his suspicions. The worldly, sophisticated Joseph seems to have the upper hand as Lady Teazle, seemingly struggling with his logic, sums up the argument: "So—so—then I perceive that your prescription is that I must sin in my own Defence—and part with my virtue to preserve my Reputation." Joseph is sure he has won a convert until Lady Teazle, in a surprise turn, replies: "Well certainly this is the oddest Doctrine—and the newest Receipt [recipe] for avoiding Calumny." When Joseph hypocritically claims that he has "too much honour" to mislead her, she retorts bluntly that they should leave honor out of the discussion. She adds that if she were ever driven to infidelity, "It would be by Sir Peter's ill usage—sooner than your honorable Logic after all." In these speeches, Lady Teazle shows an unexpected perspicacity and gains in dignity. Reversing the balance of power, she, not Joseph, attains the upper hand.

In an unexpected complication, Sir Peter is announced. Lady Teazle hides behind a screen, and Joseph pretends to read. What follows is, of course, fraught with dramatic irony from the moment that Sir Peter praises Joseph for his studiousness and for making "even the screen a source of knowledge" to Sir Peter's complaining to Joseph about Lady Teazle's supposed attachment to Charles. The dramatic irony intensifies as Sir Peter talks about giving Lady Teazle more of the financial independence she desires and about Joseph's courtship of Maria—two topics that Joseph does not want Lady Teazle to overhear.

In another surprise complication, Charles is announced next. Sir Peter insists that Joseph question Charles about his involvement with Lady Teazle while Sir Peter hides and listens. To prevent Sir Peter from stepping behind the screen and finding Lady Teazle, Joseph quickly invents a story about "a little French milliner" hiding there. In one of those farcical complications that comedy thrives on, Sir Peter thereupon hides in a closet at the other side of the stage.

The conversation that follows is overheard by both the Teazles, and the audience is keenly aware of how the speeches must strike them as well as the person addressed. Joseph unctuously reprimands Charles for making Sir Peter uneasy, but Charles, blunt as usual, refers to Joseph's relations with Lady Teazle. When Joseph can bear no more, he reveals that Sir Peter is listening in that very room, and Charles pulls Sir Peter from his hiding place. But ironically, Sir Peter remains obtuse, for although he assumes that Charles has cleared himself, he fails to grasp what has been said about Lady Teazle and Joseph.

The announcement of yet another arrival, Lady Sneerwell, takes Joseph off stage, leaving Sir Peter and Charles seemingly alone together. The motivation of the two in the following sequence is brilliantly conceived. Sir Peter chides Charles for not being more like his brother, a "noble" man of sentiment. But Charles finds Joseph "too moral by half," and Sir Peter, to show that Joseph is not so chaste after all, cannot resist mentioning the little French milliner. Charles, brushing aside Sir Peter's protests, immediately proceeds to look behind the screen, thereby producing the play's greatest dramatic moment:

> CHARLES SURFACE: O egad! we'll have a peep at the little Milliner—
> SIR PETER: Not for the world—Joseph—will never forgive me—
> CHARLES SURFACE: I'll stand by you—
> SIR PETER: [*Strug(g)ling with Charles*] OOds! here he is . . .
> [*Surface enters just as* CHARLES *throws down the Screen.*]
> CHARLES SURFACE: Lady Teazle! by all that's wonderfull!
> SIR PETER: Lady Teazle! by all that's Horrible!

The revelations and resulting insights are indeed deliciously complex. Charles and Sir Peter are surprised to find not a French milliner but Lady Teazle. Whereas Charles finds this merely "wonderful"—inspiring wonder, extraordinary—Sir Peter finds it "horrible" because now for the first time he feels betrayed by Joseph and his wife. These two, in turn, realize that they have been found out—Lady Teazle for being in Joseph's house and Joseph for having spun his web of lies. The scene as a whole has been built up brilliantly to this one moment when the screen is, in every sense, removed. In fact, the screen and the closet, like Charles's family portraits, are not merely stage props but take on a rich symbolic meaning. The screen is the perfect image for the hiding and deception that have been going on, the closet an equally good image for Sir Peter's blindness. The point is emphasized when Charles, the only frank and open person present, expresses his surprise at all the hide-and-seek and then turns specifically to Sir Peter, saying "tho' I found you in the Dark—perhaps you are not so now—"

The time has come for further explanations. Joseph produces an incoherent story to explain Lady Teazle's presence in his house. But Lady Teazle retains her new integrity and in her second great moment in the scene bluntly declares that the story is untrue, that Joseph is a hypocrite, and that she was almost misled by him. When Joseph, trying to stop her, exclaims, "The Woman's mad—," she retorts, "No Sir—she has re-cover'd her Senses." She has seen through Joseph's falseness, and she has also come to appreciate her husband, whose generous offer of a financial settlement she has overheard. In these respects, the screen scene is a trial of Lady Teazle's character, just as the picture scene is a trial of Charles's.

Act V brings the last of the expected tests, Sir Oliver's disguising himself as Mr. Stanley and asking Joseph for charity. The outcome is predictable. In reply to "Mr. Stanley's" pleas, Joseph claims he has no money and ironically blames his uncle Oliver for keeping him short. The interview is brief and does not compete with the more elaborate picture and screen scenes. It merely ends with Joseph, who has visibly failed his test, ironically priding himself on having managed to appear charitable without cost to himself.

The expected final confrontation between the two Surface brothers and their uncle is tantalizingly delayed by the return of the scandalmongers in Act V, scene 2. They are eager to discuss "Sir Peter's Discovery," and most of them are amusingly misinformed. Indeed, they launch an elaborate story about Sir Peter's being wounded in a duel, until the entrance of Sir Peter gives the lie to their fabrications. The scene that follows shows the scandalmongers at their worst and Sir Peter at his best. When the gossipers insultingly commiserate with Sir Peter and imply that everyone will be laughing at him, Sir Peter, outraged, throws them out of his house, calling them precisely what they are: "Fiends—Vipers!—Furies!—Oh that their own Venom would choak them—" This invective, outright name-calling, is in obvious contrast to their insidious remarks. It clears the air of their verbal miasma and disposes of them as they deserve.

The last scene, in Joseph's library, shows Lady Sneerwell and Joseph making a final effort to prevent the match between Charles and Maria. Snake is to perjure himself by saying that Charles has made binding promises to Lady Sneerwell. This new intrigue is interrupted by a knocking off stage that makes Joseph believe that Sir Oliver has finally arrived. But still the ultimate revelation is delayed. For when Sir Oliver enters, Joseph sees before him only his poor relative Stanley, and Charles, who joins him, sees only *his* Mr.

Premium. The brothers argue about the name and agree only that the man must leave. Ironically, both are, according to the stage directions, "forcing Sir Oliver out" when the sudden entrance of Sir Peter, Lady Teazle, Maria, and Rowley ends their misconceptions.

The moment of insight comes simultaneously to both brothers and leaves them almost speechless. It is followed by Sir Oliver's explicit judgments, which parallel Sir Peter's judgments of the scandalmongers in the preceding scene. Sir Oliver harshly condemns Joseph for his falseness and lack of benevolence and more gently reprimands Charles for the cavalier treatment of his ancestors. The brothers remain quite consistent: Joseph makes excuses, whereas Charles denies nothing and is pleased to find his uncle. His response confirms what one has suspected all along, that Charles has more family feeling than he showed in the picture scene.

Once Sir Oliver and Charles are reconciled, Lady Teazle tries to reconcile Charles and Maria. But here, in the very last moment, one more complication arises as Maria believes that Lady Sneerwell has a prior claim on Charles. Lady Sneerwell appears and makes her accusation; Charles is baffled; Joseph claims he has proof of his brother's misdeeds. But when Snake enters, he refuses to confirm Joseph's story; with disarming frankness, Snake reveals that although he was paid well for his lying, he is being paid better to tell the truth.

The final resolutions are now at hand. Lady Teazle officially resigns from "the scandalous college," and she and Sir Peter are reconciled. Lady Sneerwell sweeps out, uttering suitable curses, and is followed by Joseph, who remains a hypocrite to the end. And finally, Maria and a reformed Charles are united. There is no sentimental lingering over forgiveness, repentance, or other heart-throbbing moments, just a satisfactory rounding off of the action once the truth is out.

The plot of *The School for Scandal* is remarkable not only for its extraordinary complications and surprise turns, nor merely for the skillful intertwining of the Surface, Teazle, and scandalmonger intrigues, but also for the striking theatrical scenes that make one high point follow the other. Yet whereas the scenes are more vivid still than those of Sheridan's earlier plays, the characters are less flamboyant, less startlingly eccentric. On the other hand, many are more complex than Sheridan's earlier creations.

Joseph and Charles Surface present a fascinating study in contrasts. True to their name of *Surface*, each is flawed in his own way, for Joseph pretends to be much better than he is, and Charles appears much worse than he is. The play emphasizes their differences, but in fact they are two extremes of the same type: the good-natured man or man of sentiment whom Sheridan's contemporaries so admired and whom Sheridan so consistently ridiculed.

Joseph is the hypocrite *par excellence*—a favorite in social comedy since Molière's *Tartuffe*. One of the chief manipulators in the play, he embarks on any intrigue that seems to be to his advantage. Yet he is never a serious threat, and the fun of his scenes comes from watching him unctuously acting out his masquerades, whether as high-minded brother, passionate suitor, or selfless friend, playing his parts with elegance and verve. At the end he is unmasked—an appropriate punishment for the hypocrite who has always tried to hide his true self.[3] But ultimately,

Joseph is unrepentant, still uttering insincere moralizings as he leaves and thereby serving as ironic comment on the world of the town, where base hypocrites are unlikely to change.

Joseph's pretense of being "a man of sentiment" gives his character an added twist. It suggests that a good deal of hypocrisy and cant were associated with the sentimentalism in vogue in Sheridan's day. Joseph lacks the two essentials of the true man of sentiment: genuine love for others (he wants Maria only for her money) and charity (he categorically rejects Mr. Stanley's plea). Ironically, Joseph is given the very selfishness and hardness of heart that the sentimentalists claimed were not part of human nature.

Whereas Joseph is too selfish, calculating, and niggardly, Charles is too lacking in self-interest, too heedless and prodigal. Significantly, he first appears on stage in the company of a friend called Careless. An immature young man, he has too much heart and not enough good sense and moderation. Charles's flaws are, however, less serious than Joseph's—they are open folly rather than hidden vice—and so he is allowed to reform, become reconciled with his family, and win his virtuous bride.

The characterization of Charles is usually regarded as less successful than that of Joseph, chiefly because his redemption, seemingly based only on his refusal to sell Sir Oliver's portrait, appears insufficiently motivated. Goldsmith's complaint about sentimental heroes would seem to apply to Charles: "If they happen to have Faults or Foibles, the Spectator is taught not only to pardon, but to applaud them, in consideration of the goodness of their hearts."[4]

Yet it is not just the retaining of the portrait that

redeems Charles but also other signs of his charity, such as his continued desire to help Mr. Stanley. The main problem with the characterization of Charles is one of execution—Sheridan's failure to dramatize a moment of awareness in which Charles recognizes that he has carried his good nature too far. Since the moments of insight of the other characters are presented so vividly, in the screen scene and the final unmaskings, the development of Charles is left strangely incomplete.

The main women of the play are familiar social comedy types. Lady Sneerwell is the fashionable lady of town society, who delights in intrigues and manipulations. As her name suggests, she specializes in malicious gossip, supposedly because she was once slandered herself. She remains consistently heartless, hypocritical, and destructive, and, like Joseph, she has no mere foibles or follies but actual vices.

In contrast to Lady Sneerwell, a woman of experience, Lady Teazle is a novice in society. She is a combination of two types: the unpolished young woman from the country and the affected society lady of the town. Her part can be—and has been—acted either as if she were an awkward rustic type, aspiring to tastes that do not suit her, or a socially ambitious lady making strenuous efforts to hide her embarrassing country origins.[5]

Unexpectedly, Lady Teazle becomes one of the play's most complex characters in that she genuinely develops. Extravagant, frivolous, and heartless at first, she follows the dictates of fashion in trying to attract a lover. But she retains her "country Prejudices" (Act II, sc. 2), the moral standards that were more strictly upheld in the country than in town, and at the moment of temptation she can see through Joseph's specious reasoning that is typical of town society. Reasserting her native sense of honor and good sense, Lady Teazle significantly rejects Joseph of her own free will, before she is forced to hide behind the screen. Having made this choice, she emerges as a more integrated and much more sympathetic woman, presumably able to take her place in society with her values intact.

Maria is the least developed of the women. The virtuous heroine, she represents the norm or ideal by which the others are judged. But she is bland, and she illustrates the sad truth that characters who are pure and perfect are less interesting than those who have foibles, follies, or vices.

Much more complex is one of the two older men, Sir Peter Teazle. He is that perennial figure of fun, December married to May. Peevish if not downright choleric, he is also a muted version of the type of old man that goes back to Roman comedy.[6] But he is presented much more in the round than one would expect from these traditional types. Sir Peter is blind and opinionated in misjudging the Surface brothers but clearsighted enough to recognize the destructiveness of the gossipers. He is at times blind about himself, as when he claims that only Lady Teazle is at fault in their quarrels, but he is also capable of self-knowledge and self-irony, for he is aware of his own ridiculous situation. He disapproves of his wife's behavior—and yet he finds her charming—and yet he refuses to admit that he is fond of her. Sir Peter is most memorable when he is most unreasonable—at the end of the great "tiff," for instance, when he is furious with Lady Teazle for nothing more than that she has kept her composure, whereas he has lost his: "I'll not bear her presuming to keep her Temper—No she may break my Heart but she shan't keep her Temper" (Act III, sc. 1). A bundle of contradictions, Sir Peter has universal human foibles.

Sir Oliver is a simpler type than Sir Peter. He is the rich uncle from abroad, and beyond that the *deus ex machina* or godlike figure of ancient drama, who in this case arrives early rather than in the last minute. His character is enlivened by the disarming foible of vanity that makes him so quickly forgive Charles. But on the whole, he is the play's authority figure, reassuring us early that the right people will be tested, shams will be unmasked, and justice will prevail.

Associated with Sir Oliver is the minor figure Moses, who helps with the testing of Charles. Moses is the stereotyped Jewish moneylender but is treated rather gently. Although he charges usurious rates and hypocritically blames his outrageous demands on a ruthless friend, he is, at least, not hypocritical about his hypocrisy. In this respect, he is an amusing intermediary figure between Joseph Surface, the total hypocrite, and Sir Oliver, the truthful man.

The remaining minor characters, the scandalmongers, are usually remembered as a group but are cleverly differentiated. Mrs. Candour, true to her name, has an irrepressible urge to be frank, and although she pretends to be good-natured, she can say only the worst about her acquaintances. Sir Benjamin Backbite and his uncle Mr. Crabtree specialize in "direct malice," and in addition, Sir Benjamin is "a pretty wit" and "a pretty Poet" (Act I, sc. 1), producing verses as ineffectual as the diminutive "pretty" suggests. Snake represents written rather than spoken slander and is used to satirize gossip columnists, who were just becoming popular.[7]

The "scandalous college" seems to have been inspired by a number of earlier plays, such as Ben Jonson's *Epicoene* (1609) with its "ladies collegiate," Molière's *The Misanthrope* with Celimène's devastating thumbnail sketches of her acquaintances, and William Congreve's *The Double Dealer* (1693) with its brief scene of gossip, full of objectionable personal remarks.[8] But Sheridan's scandal scenes are much fuller than his precursors'. The scandalmongers give a series of brilliant lecture/demonstrations, and ironically they cultivate slander as an art form that requires design, coloring, invention, and talent (Act I, sc. 1). In the first part of the play they make impertinent remarks about people with allegorical names such as Miss Gadabout and Mr. and Mrs. Honeymoon. Later they concentrate on Sir Peter's "Discovery," and the audience can relish the discrepancy between an event just shown on stage and the conflicting, vastly embellished reports. The very conception of scandalmongering both as an art of fabrication and as malicious destructiveness is an extraordinarily rich image for the falseness and heartlessness that the play associates with town society.

The diverse characters are assembled with attention to symmetry and balance. They come in couples—the two Surface brothers and their ladies, the Teazles, and the two older men, Sir Peter and Sir Oliver—all with parallel yet contrasting characters and experiences. Even the two servants contrast, Rowley being sober and upright; Charles's valet Trip, frivolous and extravagant. Yet somehow the disposition of characters seems less schematic than in Sheridan's earlier plays, perhaps because of the intermittent appearance of the scandalmongers, who suggest a crowd.

The tone of *The School for Scandal* is quite varied, ranging from the gentle, affectionate mockery of Sir Peter to the high-spirited joviality of the picture scene, and from the subtle ironies of the screen scene to the sharp ridicule of the scandalmongers. On the whole, however, there is less good-humored acceptance of eccentricities and of the absurdities of human behavior than in *The Rivals*. Instead, there is a keener sense of life's ironies, not the least of which is the fact that the false and hardhearted can continue to flourish in society. It is this sceptical, critical view of life that has probably contributed to Sheridan's reputation as a wit rather than as a humorist.

Primarily, however, it is the dialogue that accounts for Sheridan's reputation for wit. The play is chiefly remembered for its brilliant witticisms, most of which occur in the scandal scenes. Some of these are elegantly concise, such as Mrs. Candour's cutting description of a widow who "got rid of her Dropsy and recover'd her shape in the most surprising manner" (Act I, sc. 1) with its innuendo about illegitimate childbirth. Others are more elaborate, such as Sir Benjamin's sketch of an elderly lady's use of cosmetics: "—come—come it is not that she paints so ill—but when she has finish'd her Face she joins it on so badly to her Neck that she looks like a mended Statue in which the Connoisseur sees at once that the Head's so modern tho' the Trunk's antique" (Act II, sc. 2). It is complex images such as this that no doubt made Sheridan's contemporaries see him as a rival of Congreve.[9]

But much of the dialogue is less mannered and marvelously captures the rhythms of colloquial speech. "Lady Teazle—Lady Teazle I'll not bear it." "Sir Peter—Sir Peter you—may bear it or not as you please, but I ought to have my own way in every thing, and what's more, I will too—" (Act II, sc. 1) marks the beginning of the Teazles' first squabble. "No hang it, I'll not part with poor Noll—The Old Fellow has been very good to me, and Egad I'll keep his Picture, while I've a Room to put it in" is Charles Surface's very direct reply to Sir Oliver's blunt "I suppose your Uncle Oliver goes with the rest of the Lumber" (Act IV, sc. 1). The understated colloquial speeches of this scene are in sharp contrast to the inflated speeches of Joseph when he is tested by Sir Oliver.

In fact, not only is there a considerable range of styles in the play but also a significant differentiation between two sets of speakers. On the one hand are those who speak elaborately. These are the spreaders of falsehood, who either becloud the issue with sententious generalities, as does Joseph, or who bedazzle their listeners with clever but unfounded gossip, as do the scandalmongers. On the other hand are those who speak plainly—Charles, Sir Oliver, Maria, and, for the most part, Rowley. There is something refreshingly direct in Sir Oliver's early comment about Joseph— "if he salutes me with a scrap of morality in his mouth I shall be sick directly" (Act II, sc. 3)—and in Sir Peter's "Leave my House" as he throws the scandalmongers out (Act V, sc. 2). And at the moment of truth, the language is always starkly simple: Charles's "Lady Teazle! by all that's wonderfull!" followed by Sir Peter's "Lady Teazle! by all that's Horrible!" (Act IV, sc. 3), or Joseph's and Charles's calling each other's name when they recognize their uncle, followed by Joseph's "'Tis now compleat!—" and Charles's laconic "Very" (Act V, sc. 3). Sheridan, far from merely relishing witticisms, as one critic has suggested,[10] uses very different diction for hiding and for uncovering the truth.

This difference between the false and the genuine, appearances and reality, permeates the play and makes it more coherent than Sheridan's earlier pieces. The theme extends not only to the web of falsehood spun by Lady Sneerwell and Joseph and to the concern for social appearances shown by the scandalmongers, but also to the very name of the Surface brothers and even to Sir Oliver's disguises and deceptions that bring out the truth. Furthermore, linked with this theme of appearance and reality is the traditionally related one of blindness and insight. Falsehoods and appearances mislead most of the good characters, especially the Teazles, who must emerge from deception and confusion to knowledge and clarity of vision, largely about others but partly also about themselves.

*The School for Scandal* still deals with personal relationships, with the traditional themes of love's vagaries and the tensions between generations, but the conflicts are no longer simplified. The young are no longer so young and the old no longer so ridiculous as in Sheridan's earlier plays. Now both the younger and the older generation supply the fools—Charles Surface and the Teazles—while the younger set also supplies the knaves, Joseph and Lady Sneerwell. For the first time in Sheridan's plays, moreover, a benevolent older figure represents order and authority—a step toward conservatism and an acceptance of the idea of a benevolently ruled hierarchy in the universe that was widely held in the eighteenth century.

Altogether, the play echoes many ideas of its time, including some of the key values of sentimentalism. Certainly the distrust of the town and of wit as cultivated by fashionable society is among these. So is the treasuring of the good heart, which goes so far that Charles Surface's reform is not even dramatized because he has the requisite charity and capacity for feeling. Is *The School for Scandal*, then, sentimental in spite of itself, as some critics have claimed?[11]

The issue is complex. For although the town is condemned, the country is nowhere glamorized. Although wit is equated with malice, Sheridan felt free to use wit for his own purposes, if only to discredit wit. Although the good heart and charity are obviously valued, so is the need for good sense, strongly represented by Sir Oliver and Rowley. And the excesses of sentimentalism are sharply attacked, whether in the form of uncontrolled liberality or of hypocritical mouthings without genuine feeling.

In any case, the play differs from the outright sentimental comedies of its time in that there is no milking of scenes for pathos and other sentiments.[12] And yet, some of the characters, notably the Teazles, are treated with a warmth and affection not found in earlier, more acerb comedies. The play as a whole, with its great comic scenes, wit, and elegance, its sharp observations of follies and its mellow treatment of foibles, really takes the best from both the antisentimental tradition and the cult of sentiment.

From the moment *The School of Scandal* opened on May 8, 1776, at the Drury Lane theater, of which

Many strands of the intricate plot of *The School for Scandal* come together at the climactic moment when the screen falls and various deceptions come to light. In this 1777 etching of the original Drury Lane production, Lady Teazle is discovered behind the fallen screen. The hypocritical Joseph Surface is at the left; the impetuous Charles Surface and the crotchety Sir Peter Teazle, at the right. Also shown are the elaborate painted backdrops suggesting Joseph's library, the sparse furnishings, and the large forestage flanked by side boxes.

THE RAYMOND MANDER AND JOE MITCHENSON THEATRE COLLECTION

Sheridan had recently become manager, it was a huge success. It was given sixteen times during the first year and became the play most frequently staged before 1800—261 times in all.[13] Horace Walpole, who was not given to effusive praise, found the acting extraordinary, and indeed, Sheridan made the most of his actors' potentialities. Thomas King, the company's best comedian, noted for his expressive face and fidgeting, played Sir Peter Teazle. John Palmer, known for villainous parts and himself something of a hypocrite, played

Joseph Surface, while the cheerful William "Gentleman" Smith was a likeable Charles. James William Dodd, who specialized in fops, acted Sir Benjamin Backbite, and William Parsons, "the wasp to Dodd's butterfly,"[14] took the part of Crabtree. Miss Jane Pope used her deadpan delivery to good purpose for Mrs. Candour's stream of gossip. And the elegant, astringent Mrs. James Abington, in her forties, made Lady Teazle very much a lady of the town as well as giving her a womanly touch. Interestingly, Dorothy

Jordan, the next actress to play Lady Teazle, emphasized her country background and gave her a girlish
quality. Of the original cast, only Priscilla Hopkins
as Maria was weak—a fact that accounts for the absence of extensive love scenes between Maria and
Charles.[15]

In the New World, the play was first produced in
1781 in Kingston, Jamaica, by the American Company
of Comedians exiled from New York by the Revolutionary War. The following year, it was given several
amateur performances in New York by British officers
serving under Sir Henry Clinton and known as Clinton's Thespians. The first professional performance
in America was given in Baltimore in 1784. Once the
American Company of Comedians returned to the
United States in 1785, they presented their version in
New York and Baltimore with extraordinary success.
The play was found so pleasing that the new theater
in Richmond, Virginia, opened with it in October,
1786. In Philadelphia the Quakers' opposition to theatrical entertainments was circumvented by presenting
the play between the parts of "A Concert" and advertising it as "a COMIC LECTURE in five parts on
the PERNICIOUS VICE OF SCANDAL."[16]

In nineteenth-century England the comedy proved
so popular that it was given every year both in London
and in the provinces. Each period's favorite actors took
the key parts. In the first decades Charles Kemble frequently played Charles Surface. William Macready,
famous for his tragic roles, is known to have played
Joseph in 1821, 1832, and 1833; Fanny Kemble was
Lady Teazle in the early 1830s, and William Farren
became a much-loved Sir Peter. Starting in the mid-

1830s, Charles Mathews took the part of Charles and John Baldwin Buckstone that of Sir Benjamin; both could still be seen in these parts in 1876. From the mid-century on, William Henry Chippendale was a memorable Sir Peter. In some productions, Joseph Surface apparently degenerated into a melodramatic villain, and Henry Irving is credited with revitalizing the part in the 1870s, stressing Joseph's worldly, elegant side.[17] In 1872, William Farren, Jr. took over "his father's great part"[18] and continued as Sir Peter for the next quarter century. In the 1880s, Henry Beerbohm Tree began as Sir Benjamin but then moved up to Joseph. Lily Langtry played Lady Teazle in the 1880s; Mrs. Patrick Campbell did so in 1896 in a production in which William Farren junior was still Sir Peter.

In the United States the comedy also continued to be a favorite throughout the nineteenth century. Early in the period, the versatile Joseph Jefferson was said to be equally good as Sir Oliver, Charles Surface, and Crabtree. From the mid-century on, John Gilbert was a great Sir Peter. The play became a standard part of the great American repertory companies: the Boston Museum and Wallack's in New York. It was also put on almost every year at Daly's theater in New York in an adaptation that avoided frequent changes of scene by locating each act in one distinct setting: Lady Teazle's or Charles's or Joseph's or Sir Peter's rooms.

Largely because of the new interest in realistic settings, the scenes were also rearranged in English productions of the later nineteenth century. As furniture and wall treatments became increasingly elaborate, quick changes of scene became impossible. The most important realistic production of *The School for*

*Scandal* was staged in 1874 by the Bancrofts and T. W. Robertson. They vividly reinforced Sheridan's characterization by making the sets for Charles's room colorful and festive; for Joseph's, somber, massive, and ostentatious.[19]

Twentieth-century productions usually treated the play as a period piece—for better and for worse—but also managed to attract outstanding casts. Ben Greet, founder and director of the Old Vic Shakespeare Repertory Company, frequently produced the play and continued in the part of Sir Peter into the 1920s. An ambitious version of 1929 featured Angela Baddeley as a tomboyish Lady Teazle and was praised for Arthur Hambling's sets, said to be unequalled as a period piece.[20] The 1933 Old Vic version had a noteworthy cast: Roger Livesey gave Joseph Surface "more oddity and depth" than expected; Peggy Ashcroft was "a very elegant, graceful, and mannered" Lady Teazle; and Alistair Sims made a memorable Crabtree.[21]

In 1937, Tyrone Guthrie combined the period-piece realism of the sets with highly stylized ballet-like movements by the actors. His remarkable cast included John Gielgud as Joseph, Michael Redgrave as Charles, Alec Guinness as Snake, and Peggy Ashcroft as Lady Teazle, repeating her 1933 part. Equally stylized was the Old Vic version of 1949, in which Laurence Olivier was a sensitive, wistful Sir Peter and Vivien Leigh a vivacious, exquisite Lady Teazle, looking like a Thomas Gainsborough portrait. The sumptuous Cecil Beaton sets made the production visually "enchanting"[22] and must have been a special delight as a contrast to the drabness of English life during the economic austerity that followed World War II.

Although there were intelligent revivals by Donald

Wolfit in 1953 and by Margaret Webster directing the Birmingham Repertory Theatre in 1960, the most important production of recent times was undoubtedly the one directed by John Gielgud in 1962. Against a series of backdrops suggested by eighteenth-century prints, Sir Ralph Richardson was a "justly rotund, ripe and heartfelt Sir Peter," John Neville was an elegantly villainous Joseph Surface, and Margaret Rutherford won high praise for her Mrs. Candour, especially for "her glee in sniffing the sweet incense of some wrecked reputation."[23] With a slightly different cast, this elegant, polished production also toured the United States.

Most modern English productions tended to prettify the play, offering a nostalgic view of a more elegant and witty age. Significantly, the 1949 Olivier-Vivien Leigh version reminded one reviewer of "a toy theater."[24] Only a few directors tried a fresh approach. In 1937, the play was given in modern dress, using modern slang. More importantly, in 1968 in Nottingham and again in 1972 in London, Jonathan Miller, while keeping the eighteenth-century settings, made the characters into second-rate provincials, placed them into sordid settings inspired by William Hogarth rather than Gainsborough, and altogether emphasized "the grime and squalor" of eighteenth-century life.[25] Lady Sneerwell looked "grotesquely balding" without her wig as she came out of her "dank boudoir," her maid was visibly pregnant, and Charles's carousing was shown as a beery brawl. Although this new approach had considerable shock value, most critics found it wrongheaded in concentrating on a social realism not found in the original and in sacrificing the comedy.[26]

In the United States the play was kept on the stage

in the early twentieth century by Otis Skinner, who played Charles Surface, and in the mid-twenties in the elaborate versions by Mrs. Samuel Insull and by George C. Tyler. But it was Ethel Barrymore who most effectively kept the comedy on the American stage. In 1923 she headed the cast of The Players Club revival and managed subtly to combine the fine

Sir John Gielgud directed an elegant revival of *The School for Scandal* in 1962. Above, the scandalmongers, led by Mrs. Candour (Margaret Rutherford), are gleefully wrecking reputations. Left, Lady Teazle hides behind the screen while the urbanely false Joseph Surface (John Neville) tries to distract the attention of the unsuspecting Sir Peter Teazle (Ralph Richardson).

ANGUS MCBEAN PHOTOGRAPHS, HARVARD THEATRE COLLECTION

town lady and the wholesome country girl in her Lady Teazle. In 1931 she directed a major production, both in New York and on tour. Brooks Atkinson praised her in the part of Lady Teazle as "a stunning figure in the bravura costumes of the period" and found that "she sweeps through her part with the poise, reserve, and splendor of a lady."[27] And in 1940

Ethel Barrymore brought the play to many East Coast communities in a season of summer stock.

The first New York production since 1931, at the Theater de Lys in 1953, suggests some of the problems found in American performances. Apparently the acting styles were mixed and "the accents range[d] from Brooklyn to the Bronx." The actors were also criticized for being "unable to portray sin with elegance and distinction."[28] In contrast, elegance and distinction are just what characterized John Gielgud's English version, which toured various American cities late in 1962 and came to New York in 1963. One critic found the cast even stronger than in London, for Gielgud, replacing John Neville and repeating the part of Joseph he had played in 1937, gave a "silken, yet cutting performance," while Geraldine McEwan, replacing Anna Massey, made Lady Teazle mischievous, brittle, sparkling, and warm in turn. The reviewer concluded that "the bloom is still on *The School for Scandal* almost two centuries after it was written."[29]

Early in the sixties, a native American version also proved that "the bloom is still on." The APA production, directed by Ellis Rabb, began in repertory in various cities and universities, and eventually came to New York in 1966. Rosemary Harris made a delightful Lady Teazle, more tomboyish and countrified than in Ethel Barrymore's portrayal, and Helen Hayes joined the company as an irrepressible Mrs. Candour.[30] Other performances have followed in the New World: in Stratford, Ontario, in 1970, directed by Michael Langham and praised for its style as well as ensemble work; in New York in 1972 in a weaker version given by the City Center Acting Company, associated with the Drama Division of Julliard; and, most recently, in

Minneapolis in 1974. None of these had the polish of the best English versions nor attempted a fresh approach. Yet, together with the countless amateur and college performances throughout the century, they attest to the play's inexhaustible appeal on the stage.

## The Critic

In his last major comedy, *The Critic; or, A Tragedy Rehearsed* (1779), Sheridan turned to the world of the theater, with which he himself had been deeply involved for the preceding five years. The play is a breezy combination of social comedy, mocking various types of people associated with the theater, and burlesque in the form of an atrocious "virgin tragedy" that ridicules pretentious playwriting and incompetent acting. Furthermore, full use is made of spectacle, which had come into vogue in the late 1770s. Although *The Critic* was an "afterpiece," performed after the main play of the evening, it is quite elaborate, with three acts and a play-within-a-play. It is a delightful spoof, spiced with satire, and ending with an unexpected touch of feeling.

For his material, Sheridan naturally drew on his own experiences as a playwright and, more recently, as manager of the Drury Lane theater. He also found a model in the Duke of Buckingham's *The Rehearsal* (1671), a burlesque or parody of the heroic plays of his contemporaries that Buckingham considered pre-

tentious and absurd, and in several subsequent "rehearsal plays."[1] In addition, Sheridan drew on a contemporary event, the threat of a combined Spanish
and French invasion in the summer of 1779 that found
England militarily unprepared but that aroused pa-
triotic feelings and revived public interest in the
Spanish Armada of 1588.[2]

The action of the first act of *The Critic* is simple,
as if Sheridan had had his fill of the complicated
intrigues of *The Rivals* and *The School for Scandal*.
A number of theater people gather at the house of
Mr. and Mrs. Dangle, each reveals his or her interests
as well as his or her follies or foibles, and some of them
eventually go to the theater to see a play in rehearsal.
Not one of them is a creative genius—all are mere
hangers-on that the theater seems to produce in all
ages.

Mr. Dangle is the self-styled patron, a busybody
who prides himself on using his influence to have a
play produced, get an actor a part, or obtain tickets
for his friends. He is so absorbed in theatrical affairs
that he pays no attention to the national emergency,
the imminent arrival of an enemy fleet. Mrs. Dangle
scolds him for his lack of concern about public affairs
and calls him "a mock Maecenas to second-hand authors," Maecenas being the great patron of ancient
Rome. With unconscious irony, Dangle reveals the
futility of his endeavors by boasting that "sometimes
of a morning I have a dozen people call on me at
breakfast time, whose faces I never saw before, nor
ever desire to see again."

Soon the Dangles are joined by Mr. Sneer, a critic
who never has a good word for anyone but whose
tastes are questionable, to judge by the execrable-

sounding plays he touts. In vivid contrast to the enthusiastic Dangle, who loves every aspect of the theater, Sneer lives up to his name by being consistently sharp-tongued, sarcastic, and denigrating. Yet his cutting remarks are often witty, and he has a certain elegance.

Next to arrive is Sir Fretful Plagiary, a proud but ineffectual playwright. Both the prevalence of literary theft and the vanity of playwrights are ridiculed—the latter as he eagerly asks for advice about his play but is deeply offended when it is offered. Still, Sir Fretful is not wholly a fool, for he sees through his supposed friends and knows that he can always count on "one damn'd good natur'd friend or another" to transmit a bad review (Act I, sc. 1). Vain and touchy, he is also likeable, and he is presented with a certain affection.

Sir Fretful Plagiary was modeled on the playwright Richard Cumberland, with whom Sheridan was on terms of friendly enmity. Several topical jokes went into the character of Sir Fretful, especially his worry that if he sent his play to Drury Lane, the manager, a playwright himself, might steal the material—the manager being Sheridan himself. Furthermore, Dangle and Sneer play a trick on Sir Fretful that David Garrick once reputedly played on Cumberland: reading a nonexistent damning review just to see the thin-skinned author squirm.[3] But Sir Fretful is more than a portrait of a particular playwright; he embodies the combination of conceit and insecurity that is typical of many aspiring authors.

The Italian singers who arrive to ask Mr. Dangle's protection in scene 2 of Act I at first seem extraneous and far-fetched. But they, too, belong to the theater and are, in fact, the first actual entertainers to appear.

Like the patron, critic, and playwright introduced before them, they are second-raters. Their very names indicate as much: Pasticcio suggests a pastiche or mere imitation of an artist's style, and Ritornello, a "little return," perhaps something *déjà vu* or already familiar. The chaotic scene in which Mrs. Dangle cannot understand either the Italian singers or their French interpreter ridicules the widespread English admiration for foreign art regardless of whether the audience can understand it. For a period that believed, with Alexander Pope, that "the sound must be an echo to the sense" (*An Essay on Criticism*, Part I, l. 365), there was something absurd about the vogue of Italian opera and other incomprehensible foreign imports.

Mr. Puff, the last and most vivid theatrical figure to appear in Mr. Dangle's house, is a "puffer" or eighteenth-century version of the publicity agent. Mr. Puff explains his professional techniques with great gusto. The puff direct, puff preliminary, puff collateral, puff collusive, and puff oblique all have their special traits, ranging from direct praise to dire warnings that arouse the public's interest. All the puffs share the elements of exaggeration and manipulation of the public—not so different from the techniques of modern advertising.

Mr. Puff has an engaging flair but is clearly an out-and-out fraud. He shamelessly admits that he supported himself for several years by writing hard-luck stories in the newspapers and getting money from charitable readers. Sheridan's audience was horrified by Puff's hypocritical appeal to the public's humanitarianism.[4] Apparently they did not understand that the outrageously fraudulent Mr. Puff, who turns the softheartedness or softheadedness of the sentimentalists to his own advantage, is actually another of Sheridan's salvos against the sentimental benevolence so much in vogue in his time.

The society conjured up through Dangle, Sneer, Sir Fretful, and Puff is very much a society of the town. Gossip, more or less malicious needling, and various kinds of falsehood abound. Hypocrisy is especially widespread. "Plague on't," says Dangle when Sneer is announced, but in the next breath he is "vastly glad" to see him and presents him to Mrs. Dangle with the amusingly assonant "My dear, here's Mr. Sneer." Together, they find Sir Fretful's new tragedy "execrable," but with the arrival of the author, "admirable." Dangle agrees with each of Sneer's cutting remarks about Sir Fretful with the disclaimer "tho' he's my friend" (Act I, sc. 1). Loyalty and genuine friendship are as non-existent as genuine creativity in Sheridan's theater world.

In this first act, current tastes in drama are also ridiculed, particularly the mania for the sentimental. Reading a new play, Dangle finds a stage direction that states "Bursts into tears, and exit," and assumes that the play is a tragedy. But it is "a genteel comedy," "the true sentimental, and nothing ridiculous in it from the beginning to the end." This ironic comment echoes Goldsmith's complaint, in his "Essay on the Theatre; or, A Comparison Between Laughing and Weeping Comedy," that sentimental comedy no longer ridicules follies and runs contrary to the very spirit of comedy.[5] Sneer's view that drama should be "the school of morality" and his regret that most people go to the theater only for entertainment mocks the high-minded moralizing of sentimental drama. And Dangle's lament that no *double entendre* or innuendo is now admitted—"even Vanbrugh and Congreve obliged to undergo a bungling reformation" (Act I, sc. 1)—hits at the prudish taste of genteel audiences. This last line is, moreover, fraught with self-irony; Sheridan himself had recently submitted Vanbrugh's *The Relapse* to considerable "reformation" in transforming it into *A Trip to Scarborough.* Amusingly, even Mrs. Dangle, usually the voice of common sense, shares the passion for the sentimental, thereby showing the extent of its vogue. At the same time, Mrs. Dangle's concern for England's national safety suggests that all the theatrical concerns are frivolous, superficial, and far removed from pressing realities.

Mr. Puff's "The Spanish Armada," which takes up most of Acts II and III, is a high-spirited romp, through which countless aspects of playwriting, staging, and acting are ridiculed. It is a burlesque in two senses, in parodying the genre of heroic tragedy and in treating unworthy material in an inflated manner, serious material in a low manner. As a result, it is full of surprises, absurdities, and outrageous exaggerations, each with a hidden barb that suggests a weakness in actual plays or performances.

Discernible in the welter of Puff's material are the outlines of a heroic tragedy, a serious genre that usually deals with national figures in crisis. Puff's plot concerns the forbidden love of Tilburina, daughter of the Governor of Tilbury Fort, for Don Ferolo Whiskerandos, son of the Spanish Admiral. All the hackneyed scenes of heroic tragedy are presented in suitably climactic order: a stirring prayer for victory by the English leaders; the solemn entrance of the heroine, accompanied by a confidante, to the sound of soft music; the clash between father and daughter that dramatizes the traditional conflict between love and duty; the parting of the lovers; complications as two other women vie for Don Whiskerandos; the entrance in disguise of an English hero, rival for the heroine's hand; the duel of the rivals and the death of Don Whiskerandos; the madness of the heroine *and* of her confidante; and a final allegorical procession. Thematic confusion is rife, for the heroine should presumably marry the English hero and not go mad for love of a Spaniard, and the procession of English rivers at the end has only the vaguest relation to the preceding events. Ironically, Puff alludes to Aristotle's principle that tragedy should deal with the probable rather than with the merely possible, while actually managing to create a plot that is both improbable and impossible.

In addition, there is a subplot, guaranteed to have no connection with the main plot. This secondary action features a "discovery" scene that parodies the most famous recognition scene of eighteenth-century drama in John Home's *Douglas* (1756); in Puff's play, the solemn moment is reduced to farce as the young man's name turns out to be not the sonorous "Norval" of *Douglas* but "Jenkins," and his parents are identified as former fishmongers. What this scene is doing in a heroic play about the Spanish armada never becomes clear.

Among the more general weaknesses of playwriting, mishandling of the exposition comes in for heavy satire. In the opening scene, Sir Walter Raleigh and Sir Christopher Hatton labor the obvious as they describe the state of England under Queen Elizabeth and the expected arrival of the Spanish Armada—illustrating the playwright's dilemma of having to supply the audience with information that the characters are bound to have. Later, Lord Burleigh enters and merely looks grave, thinks, nods, and exits—showing the playwright's other dilemma of wanting a character to act realistically but having to ignore the audience's need to know his thoughts and motives. The inherent absurdity of "asides" is also emphasized, as the "two nieces," the young women in love with Don Whiskerandos, first say to each other the lines that should be spoken "aside," and then launch into a long series of artificially parallel "asides."

Mishandling of stage business is also mocked. Exits are a problem: actors on their knees at prayer cannot manage a graceful departure, and the premature exit of the dead Whiskerandos makes nonsense of his rival's last words, meant to be spoken over the dead body. Stage props go wrong: the morning cannon unexpectedly goes off not once but three times. The heroine is invariably shadowed by a confidante, a piece of business that culminates in Puff's unforgettable stage direction: " 'Enter Tilburina stark mad in white satin and her confidant stark mad in white linen' "—a line that speaks volumes about the ubiquitousness of confidantes and of mad scenes in eighteenth-century drama.

The proceedings are further enlivened by the constant interplay between the characters visiting the theater and the actors in Puff's play. Puff's energetic urging, advising, cajoling, and commanding of the actors, and the actors' frequent retorts dramatize the natural conflict between the two factions. Puff, like most authors, believes that the actors are mutilating his play; the actors are displeased with their vehicle and have actually cut the passages they disliked.

A series of in-house jokes add to the complications. The Drury Lane prompter, Mr. Hopkins, appears in his own person. Earlier, in demonstrating his various "puffs," Mr. Puff gives high praise to the actors Dodd and Palmer, highest praise to the actor King: the audience was, in fact, watching Dodd play Dangle, Palmer play Sneer, and King himself play Puff. Since King had a few months earlier produced a pantomime entitled *The Prophecy; or, Queen Elizabeth at Tilbury*, this kind of joking also probably explains why the play-within-the-play is attributed to Puff and not to the playwright Sir Fretful.[6]

Puff's play and *The Critic* as a whole end in striking spectacle. Using recent advances in scene painting, scene shifting, machinery, and lighting, the Drury Lane scene designer Philip De Loutherbourg was able to create a splendid simulated sea battle ending with the destruction of the Spanish fleet. This was followed by the procession of the English rivers, led by the Thames, each carrying symbolic emblems. The musical accompaniment ranged from "Britons strike home" during the battle to George Frederick Handel's popular "Water Music" and the march from *Judas Maccabeus* during the procession.

The tone of this finale is complex. Certainly, on the one hand, there is mockery of Puff's—and presumably the contemporary audience's—naive delight in extravaganza. "Now then for my magnificence!—my battle! —my noise!—and my procession!—" cries the enthusiastic Puff, only to be immediately foiled by the inept actor playing Thames, who cannot manage to walk between the two other actors playing his banks. On the other hand, a stirring spectacle is created through the sets, machinery, lighting, and music. And ulti-

mately, the play indeed celebrates an English triumph
—the threatened Spanish and French invasion had,
after all, not materialized in 1779—and the final patri-
otic note is not entirely tongue in cheek.

Structurally, *The Critic* has a much looser, more
open form than Sheridan's previous comedies. Gone
are the parallels and contrasts among lovers, parents,
and other assorted couples. Gone, too, is the sharply
defined closed ending. No attempt is made to bring
the figures of Act I back in the finale. Obviously
enjoying the freedom of moving from high point to
high point without careful preparation, Sheridan in
this play preferred flexibility and experimentation to
working out the intricate minuet-like steps of traditional comedy.

The most memorable and delightful part of *The
Critic*, however, is its language. Never before was
Sheridan so versatile, inventive, and exuberant. The
speeches of the heroic figures are elevated into pseudo-
Shakespearean images of pretentious grandeur. In a
brilliant burlesque passage that inflates the description,
then undercuts it with an anticlimactic conclusion, Sir
Christopher Hatton conjures up the assembled armies
in terms vaguely reminiscent of *Henry V* and *Hamlet*:

> When I count o'er yon glittering lines
> Of crested warriors, where the proud steeds neigh,
> And valor-breathing trumpets shrill appeal
> Responsive vibrate on my listening ear; . . .
> When briefly all I hear or see bears stamp
> Of martial vigilance and stern defence,
> I cannot but surmise.—Forgive, my friend,
> If the conjecture's rash—I cannot but
> Surmise.—The state some danger apprehends!
>
> (ACT II)

Later, the heroine's mad scene echoes Ophelia's in *Hamlet*, with the flower images transposed into ridiculous animal images. To draw attention to the frequent echoes of Shakespeare, Sneer and Dangle remind Puff that his Beefeater's "Perdition catch my soul but I do love thee" comes from *Othello*, whereupon Puff dismisses the point with the unforgettable comment: "that's of no consequence—all that can be said is, that two people happened to hit on the same thought—And Shakespeare made use of it first, that's all" (Act III). Not only is Puff's derivativeness stressed, but the play also mocks the current Shakespeare idolatry that reached a peak with David Garrick's Shakespeare Jubilee in Stratford-upon-Avon in 1769.

Over and over, an inflating of language as fanciful as Mrs. Malaprop's outrageous slips of the tongue in *The Rivals* is combined with the unexpected intrusion of the commonplace, prosaic, or blunt that had worked so well in *The Duenna* and *The School for Scandal*. Some of the "sinking" suggests Puff's flagging genius —for instance, Tilburina's pastoral catalogue, which becomes increasingly literal-minded in its enumeration of birds and flowers, down to the subspecies of finches ("chaffinch! bullfinch! goldfinch! greenfinch!"). The lovers' parting suffers from a similar deflation:

> TILBURINA:
> Could I pursue the bias of my soul,
> All friends, all right of parents I'd disclaim,
> And thou, my Whiskerandos, should'st be father
> And mother, brother, cousin, uncle, aunt,
> And friend to me!
>
> WHISKERANDOS:
> O matchless excellence!—and must we part?

Well, if—we must—we must—and in that case,
The less is said the better.

(ACT II)

The last lapse is attributed not to Puff's ineptitude but
to the impatience of the actors, who have cut again.
Indeed, another way in which the inflated poetic diction of the heroic figures is debunked is by having a
more realistic voice break in. After Whiskerandos has
repeatedly tried his Shakespearean last line—"And
Whiskerandos quits this bustling scene/For all eter—
[nity]"—he refuses to practice further, claiming "I
can't stay dying here all night" (Act III). And Tilburina's "heart-rending woe" is greeted not only by
Dangle's sympathetic "Oh—it's too much" but also by
Sneer's unsympathetic echo: "Oh!—it is indeed" (Act
II). As in Sheridan's earlier plays, different voices are
played off against each other, and the best burlesque
effects are created by a witty shifting of styles.

The interplay between the poetic bombast of Puff's
characters and the prosaic speech of Sheridan's is one
of many signs that Sheridan continued, in *The Critic*,
to be fascinated by the themes of surface and substance, appearance and reality, illusion and truth.
Dangle, Sneer, Sir Fretful, and Puff all belong to the
world of mere surface and are full of the social pretensions dramatized in *The School for Scandal*. Sir
Fretful and Puff, vain about their plays, have some of
the personal illusions or delusions that characterized
the figures in *The Rivals*, and, in addition, Puff deals
with illusion and delusion in his "puffing." But beyond
that, the theater provides an even better setting for
these themes than the drawing rooms of the earlier
plays.

Indeed, the theater setting permitted Sheridan to

play with almost as many levels of reality as Luigi Pirandello was to do in *Six Characters in Search of an Author*. In Acts II and III, Dangle and Sneer represent the audience on stage; the playwright Puff views his creation on a stage-within-the-stage; the actors at times embody Puff's characters and at other times speak in their own voices; and the Drury Lane prompter Hopkins as well as the jokes about the actors Dodd, Palmer, and King bring in still another reality, that of actual life. Sheridan was not, however, interested in questions of identity, as Pirandello was to be, but rather in the contrasts between art and life, particularly the difference between inferior art and infinitely more fascinating, irrepressible life.

The relationship of art and life and the problem of quality in art are, in fact, also fundamental themes of *The Critic*. Early in Act I, Dangle asserts, in terms borrowed from *Hamlet*, that "the stage is 'the Mirror of Nature,' and the actors are 'the Abstract, and brief Chronicles of the Time'." Ironically, Puff's atrocious play is made to seem far removed from contemporary realities, even though it deals with the relevant topic of a Spanish invasion, and the ineffectual actors in Puff's play have no chance to serve as chronicles. But Sheridan's play, vividly dramatizing the second-rate theatrical figures, the contemporary audiences with their misguided taste, the incompetent actors, and the bad art of the theatre, does indeed provide a mirror for his society and a chronicle of his time.

*The Critic* is the last comedy Sheridan wrote. Thereafter, although he continued as manager of the Drury Lane theater, he devoted most of his energies to politics. It is remarkable that in his last comedy, whether by chance or by design, he turned away from the themes of love and the clashes between generations that had recurred in his earlier plays to his own craft and profession. He viewed both with somewhat jaundiced eyes but presented them with such irrepressible flair and wit that weak personalities were transmuted into striking characters and vapid, pretentious playwriting became part of a vivid, vital work of art.

*The Critic* was well received in the theater, especially after cuts were made following the first performances. It became one of the most popular afterpieces of its time: 131 performances were recorded before 1800.[7] Thomas King, the Drury Lane company's chief comedian, excelled as Puff, as he had as Sir Peter Teazle in *The School for Scandal*; James William Dodd, specializing in fops, played Dangle; John Palmer, known for his hypocrisy and acclaimed for his Joseph Surface, played Sneer; and William Parsons, whose forte was wheezing older men, played Sir Fretful Plagiary. Miss Jane Pope, often featured as an elderly lady and distinguished by a mannish stride and deadpan delivery, made the most of Tilburina. This much-praised cast continued to present the play at Drury Lane for more than a decade.

Although the play never achieved the popularity of *The Rivals* and *The School for Scandal* in the nineteenth century, it continued to be staged in London and the English provinces every few years. Early in the century John Liston often played Whiskerandos, and William Farren, much admired for his Sir Peter Teazle, took the part of Sir Fretful. From 1840 to 1877, more than thirty-five years, Charles Mathews, in a remarkable *tour de force*, took the double roles of Puff and Sir Fretful. Both Liston and Mathews kept the topical jokes up to date by substituting the names of their fellow actors for those of Dodd, Palmer, and King in the original text. Toward the end of the century, however, *The Critic* was staged less often and was given only with rather undistinguished casts.

On the American stage, the play never really established itself. It was first presented in New York in 1786 by the American Company of Comedians, which had just returned from its ten-year exile in Jamaica due to the War of Independence, and again in 1795. It was staged in Philadelphia in 1799-1800 and in 1813, the second time with Joseph Jefferson as Sir Fretful and Mrs. Jefferson as Mrs. Dangle. In the 1850s it could be seen repeatedly in Boston and in the 1870s occasionally at Wallack's in New York. Records for American performances are sparse,[8] however, suggesting that *The Critic* was not performed frequently.

In the twentieth century, the comedy continued to be offered in England from time to time. The Birmingham Repertory Company staged it repeatedly in the 1910s. Ben Greet included it in his Sheridan Week of 1917 and played Puff in his 1921 version in Bath. In the mid-twenties it was shown at Stratford-upon-Avon, with Puff played by James Dale, and in 1928 it was staged by Sir Nigel Playfair at The Lyric, Hammersmith, again with James Dale as Puff. The famous Abbey Theatre in Dublin gave the play two separate productions, one in 1914, following W. B. Yeats's *Kathleen Ni Houlihan*, and the other in 1935, in a version modernized by Lennox Robinson. Following the time-honored tradition, Robinson updated the topical allusions and converted the setting of the play-within-the-play to "The Stage of the Abbey Theatre."

The most important production of this century was undoubtedly the Old Vic's in 1946, shortly after

The finale of the Old Vic's *The Critic* (1946) brilliantly
captured Sheridan's playful juxtaposition of various levels
of reality. On the left, the would-be patron Dangle and
the would-be critic Sneer watch the rehearsal of their
friend Puff's play. At the right, the actors in Puff's play
are caught up in their own concerns. Above them, at the
climactic moment that is true to the spirit if not the letter
of Sheridan's comedy, the frothy Puff (Laurence Olivier)
is swept to the heavens on a cardboard wave as the scenery
disintegrates.
JOHN VICKERS

World War II, which was a triumph first in London and then in New York. Staged by the actor Miles Malleson, with scenery and costumes by Tanya Moiseiwitsch, it featured Laurence Olivier as Puff, Ralph Richardson as the silent Lord Burleigh, George Relph as Mr. Dangle, Margaret Leighton as Mrs. Dangle, and Miles Malleson as Sir Fretful Plagiary. The inventive, high-spirited production, likened by one reviewer to *Hellzapoppin*[9], culminated in an unforgettable finale in which the scenery self-destructed, and Olivier rose up to the heavens clinging precariously to a cardboard wave, only to descend a moment later on a cardboard cloud.

Although this piece of stage business is not in the original, it is a fitting culmination of Puff's ineptness and well suggests his insubstantial character. What made the evening all the more remarkable was that *The Critic* was presented as afterpiece to Sophocles' *Oedipus* and that Olivier, in an unparalleled acting feat, followed his deeply moving portrayal of Oedipus with the "bubbling froth" of Mr. Puff.[10] Without rivaling this production, the Theatre Royal in Bristol celebrated its bicentenary season in 1966 by presenting *The Critic* prior to Terence Rattigan's *Harlequinade* and convinced at least one reviewer that Sheridan's play was wittier than the modern playwright's.[11]

In the United States there were a number of twentieth-century productions, none the equal of the Old Vic's that toured here in 1946. B. Iden Payne played Puff over a long span of years—in 1915 in New York, in a production distinguished by cubist scenery; in 1928-29 in Chicago; and eventually in 1950 at the University of Texas, where he also directed the play to mark his over fifty years of acting. In 1925, the Neighborhood Theater of New York featured Whitford Kane as Dangle; amusingly, Dorothy Sands as Confidante stole the show, suggesting the comic possibilities of even very minor acting parts. Whitford Kane continued to play in *The Critic*—as Sir Walter Raleigh in the 1928-29 Chicago version and again as Dangle in 1936 in Newport.

Since then, however, apart from one production in Philadelphia in 1966, the play has been seen in America primarily in amateur and college productions: at Harvard (1938), the University of Michigan (1940), Vassar (1953), Smith College (1954), and the Stanford Summer Theater (1965). The charming Smith College Faculty Show of 1954, directed by James H. Durbin, Jr., had the subtitle "Considerably After Sheridan," suggesting the play's enormous potential for improvising as well as for high-spirited acting that no doubt accounts for its continued appeal, at least to literate audiences.

# CONCLUSION

Goldsmith and Sheridan are important for more than restoring "laughing comedy" to the stage of their time. Their best plays have a timeless quality; they are enormous fun—the very essence of comedy. Indeed, the general verve, the variety of comic effects, and the range of follies or foibles seen within each play are equaled by few other comedies of any age.

Although Goldsmith and Sheridan are often mentioned together, they differed from each other in significant ways and in some respects even differed from play to play. Most fundamentally, Goldsmith was a conservative, sympathizing with the older generation, upholding parental authority and the accepted values of his society, whereas Sheridan, especially in his earlier plays, was an irreverent, questioning spirit, sympathizing with the young and mocking authoritarianism in the family as well as in society. In his last two plays, Sheridan was no longer so concerned with the conflict between generations, and he introduced an older authority figure, Sir Oliver, in *The School for Scandal*. But in this play he continued to question the values of society, and in *The Critic*, he ridiculed the theatrical society and the artistic standards of his day.

A more frequently mentioned difference—that Goldsmith specialized in humor whereas Sheridan specialized in wit—needs qualification. For there are strong elements of witty social comedy and verbal wit in Goldsmith's *The Good-Natured Man*, and of humor in Sheridan's *The Rivals*. Indeed, *The Rivals*, with its amusing eccentrics and farcical antics, is closer to *The Good-Natured Man* than to *The School for Scandal*. Only in their later plays does the distinction hold, for humor is predominant in *She Stoops to Conquer* and wit in *The School for Scandal*. Interestingly enough, Goldsmith toned down his stylistic virtuosity in *She Stoops to Conquer* whereas Sheridan developed his versatility increasingly in *The Duenna* and *The School for Scandal*, culminating in the witty verbal pyrotechnics of *The Critic*.

Literary critics have not always been kind to Goldsmith and Sheridan. The main charge, often repeated, is that although their plays are ostensibly antisentimental, they are sentimental at the core.[1] Yet, to do justice to the plays, we ought to return to the distinctions about sentimentalism drawn earlier.[2] If the term "sentimental" refers to the values upheld, then Goldsmith and Sheridan undeniably accepted some of the values associated with the cult of sentiment. But they coupled these with other values. They believed in the good heart and charity provided that they were checked by good sense and prudence. They valued feeling provided that it did not degenerate into emotional excesses that led to unhappiness. And they saw clearly that among sentimentalists, as among other types, shams and humbugs could abound. These views would seem to be balanced, moderate, humane, and clear-sighted—hardly open to the charge of excessive softness of heart or of head.

If the term "sentimental" refers to the milking of scenes for pity and admiration not justified by the circumstances, then, as we have seen, Sheridan was very seldom and Goldsmith almost never sentimental. On the other hand, their attitudes toward their creations were often tinged with sentiment. Both Goldsmith and Sheridan had a certain affection for their characters, especially their eccentrics. Unfriendly critics may feel that this affection takes the bite out of the characterizations, but it could also be argued that the best characters—Mr. Hardcastle, Sir Anthony Absolute, Sir Peter Teazle—are rounder, mellower, and less brittle than their counterparts in earlier comedies.

Another criticism leveled against the two playwrights is that their plays are too healthy, too innocent, too "safe." Perhaps it is true that *She Stoops to Conquer*, especially, is full of healthy, innocent fun, but we should recall that comedy is traditionally a celebration of life,[3] and that there is surely room for "the theater of kindness"[4] as well as the theater of cruelty, for a theater of sanity as well as a theater of the absurd. As for Louis Kronenberger's witty complaint that *The School for Scandal* appears to deal with improprieties but permits nothing really to happen (no seduction, no cuckolding), and that mere gossip replaces the probing into sin of earlier comedies,[5] perhaps we should consider that the flaws and values of a character can be revealed as clearly by a flirtation as by a seduction, by words as by deeds.

Although nothing really happens, in another sense, everything happens.

In any case, regardless of the strictures of some critics, Goldsmith's and Sheridan's plays have been extraordinarily effective on the stage. The major comedies, applauded in their own day, became so popular during the nineteenth century that they were performed almost as often as Shakespeare's. In the later nineteenth century *She Stoops to Conquer*, *The Rivals*, and *The School for Scandal* became the mainstays of repertory companies on both sides of the Atlantic and came to be featured as "the glorious old comedies."[6] Although all three plays ran the danger of becoming dusty period pieces in second-rate performances—Henry James warned as early as 1874 that *The School for Scandal* was becoming "an historical relic, and ethnological monument"[7]—they survived even this threat.

Goldsmith's and Sheridan's best comedies have, in fact, remained a challenge for outstanding actors and directors of modern times. Especially in the years following World War II, the brilliant English productions of *The Rivals* (1945), *The Critic* (1946), *She Stoops to Conquer* (1949), and *The School for Scandal* (1949) caused the plays to be recognized as cultural treasures and contributed to a revival of national pride at a time of drab austerity. Since then *The School for Scandal* has been kept vividly on the stage by the elegant John Gielgud production of 1962-63 and the disturbing Jonathan Miller production of 1972; *She Stoops to Conquer*, by the zestful 1969 version with Tom Courtenay. Although modern American productions have often lacked the polish of the English, Maurice Evans's *She Stoops to Conquer* with Burl

Ives as Squire Hardcastle, Eva Le Gallienne's *The Rivals* with Bobby Clark as Acres, and the various versions of *The School for Scandal* with Ethel Barrymore as Lady Teazle have had great strengths of their own.

Goldsmith and Sheridan wrote their plays for the stage and not for the study. The continued vitality of the comedies is, surely, a remarkable achievement.

# NOTES

## GOLDSMITH, SHERIDAN, AND THEIR WORLD

1. A. Lytton Sells, *Oliver Goldsmith: His Life and Works* (London and New York, 1974), pp. 28–29.

2. Thomas Moore, *Memoirs of the Life of the Rt. Hon. Richard Brinsley Sheridan* (1858), (New York, 1968), pp. 35–78; Madeleine Bingham, *Sheridan: The Track of a Comet* (New York, 1972), pp. 54–115.

3. Bingham, p. 229 ff.

4. Ibid., p. 153.

5. *Boswell's Life of Johnson*, ed. Chauncey Brewster Tinker (New York, 1933), Vol. II, p. 86.

6. Arthur Sherbo, *English Sentimental Drama* (East Lansing, Michigan, 1957), pp. 15–99, *passim*.

7. Arthur Friedman, ed., *Collected Works of Oliver Goldsmith*, Vol. I (Oxford, 1966), pp. 293–294.

8. "Prologue by the Author, Spoken on the Tenth Night," in Cecil Price, *The Dramatic Works of Richard Brinsley Sheridan*, Vol. I (Oxford, 1973), p. 74.

9. Raymond Mander and Joe Mitchenson, *A Picture History of the British Theatre* (London, 1957), p. 32 ff.

10. Richard Leacroft, *The Development of the English Playhouse* (Ithaca, New York, 1973), pp. 118–126; Sybil Rosenfeld, *A Short History of Scene Design in Great Britain* (Oxford, 1973), pp. 80–85.

11. Allardyce Nicoll, *A History of English Drama: 1660–1900*, Vol. III (Cambridge, 1927), pp. 117–119; Harry William Pedicord, *The Theatrical Public in the Time of Garrick* (Carbondale, Ill., 1954), pp. 144–151.

12. Friedman, Vol. V, p. 90.

13. Bingham, pp. 159–160.

## THE GOOD-NATURED MAN

1. Quoted in Ronald Hastings, "In the Laughter Tradition," *The Daily Telegraph*, November 13, 1971, p. 11.

2. Byron Gassman, "French Sources of Goldsmith's *The Good-Natured Man*," *Philological Quarterly* 39 (1960): 59–62; A. Lytton Sells, *Oliver Goldsmith: His Life and Works* (London and New York, 1974), pp. 329–331.

3. Robert Heilman, "The Sentimentalism of Goldsmith's *Good-Natured Man*," in *Studies for William A. Read* (Baton Rouge, 1940), p. 246.

4. George E. Duckworth, *The Nature of Roman Comedy* (Princeton, 1952), pp. 237–242.

5. See above, p. 16.

6. *Boswell's Life of Johnson*, ed. Chauncey Brewster Tinker (New York, 1933), Vol. I, p. 367.

7. David Augustin de Brueys' *L'Important* (1694); see Gassman, pp. 59–62.

8. Friedman, Vol. V, pp. 6–7.

9. Robert H. Hopkins, *The True Genius of Oliver Goldsmith* (Baltimore, 1969), p. 40 ff.

10. Ricardo Quintana, *Oliver Goldsmith: A Georgian Study* (New York, 1967), p. 150.

11. Friedman, pp. 4–7.

12. *The Good-Natured Man* programme folder, Theater Collection, New York Public Library at Lincoln Center, New York City.

13. Jeremy Kingston, *Punch*, December 22, 1971, p. 879.

14. Quoted in Hastings, p. 11.

## SHE STOOPS TO CONQUER

1. Brooks Atkinson, *New York Times*, Dec. 29, 1949, p. 21.

2. *Boswell's Life of Johnson*, ed. Chauncey Brewster Tinker (New York, 1933), Vol. I, p. 498.

3. A. Lytton Sells, *Oliver Goldsmith: His Life and Works* (London and New York, 1974), pp. 28–29. See above, p. 6.

4. See above, p. 16.

5. Ricardo Quintana, "Goldsmith's Achievement as Dramatist," *University of Toronto Quarterly* 34 (1965): 171.

6. George E. Duckworth, *The Nature of Roman Comedy* (Princeton, 1952), pp. 237–242.

7. See William W. Appleton, "The Double Gallant in Eighteenth-Century Comedy," in *English Writers of the Eighteenth Century*, ed. John Middendorf (New York, 1971), pp. 145–157.

8. Louis Kronenberger, *The Thread of Laughter* (New York, 1952), pp. 189, 191.

9. See Karl Eichenberger, *Oliver Goldsmith: Das Komische in den Werken seiner Reifeperiode* (Bern, 1954), pp. 65–66.

10. Diggory was apparently played as "the perfect Shakespearean clown" in the 1960 Phoenix Theater production; see Brooks Atkinson, *New York Times*, Nov. 15, 1960, p. 36.

11. Arthur Friedman, ed., *Collected Works of Oliver Goldsmith*, Vol. V (Oxford, 1966), pp. 88–89.

12. Ibid., p. 90.

13. George H. Nettleton, "Sheridan's Introduction to the American Stage," *PMLA* 65 (1950): 171; Clara Marie Behringer, "A Production Prompt Book for *She Stoops to Conquer*," unpublished MA thesis, University of Michigan, 1944, p. 83.

14. Behringer, pp. 106–108; *She Stoops to Conquer* programme folder, Theater Collection, New York Public Library at Lincoln Center, New York.

15. Behringer, pp. 89–90.

16. *New York Times*, April 6, 1886.

17. Charles Morgan, reporting from London in the *New York Times*, Sept. 2, 1928.

18. Michael Billington, *Plays and Players*, 16 (1969): 52; Clive Barnes, *New York Times*, Aug. 18, 1969, p. 28; report of Professor Martha England, Queens College of the City University of New York.

19. *New York Times*, Dec. 29, 1949, p. 21.

20. Howard Taubman, *New York Times*, Nov. 2, 1960, p. 42.

21. Unidentified review, May 22, 1974, *Chips 'n' Ale* folder, Theater Collection, New York Public Library at Lincoln Center, New York City.

## THE RIVALS

1. "Prologue by the Author, Spoken on the Tenth Night," in Cecil Price, *The Dramatic Works of Richard Brinsley Sheridan*, Vol. I (Oxford, 1973), p. 74; all further references in the text are to this edition.

2. Thomas Moore, *Memoirs of the Life of the Rt. Hon. Richard Brinsley Sheridan (1858)*, (New York, 1968), pp. 35–78; Madeleine Bingham, *Sheridan: The Track of a Comet* (New York, 1972), pp. 54–115. See also above, pp. 10–11.

3. Jack D. Durant, *Richard Brinsley Sheridan* (Boston, 1975), pp. 68–69.

4. See above, p. 25.

5. Otto Reinert, ed. *An Anthology of Drama* (Boston, 1964), p. 383.

6. See William W. Appleton, "The Double Gallant in Eighteenth Century Comedy," in *English Writers of the Eighteenth Century*, ed. John H. Middendorf (New York, 1971), pp. 145–157.

7. Durant, pp. 79–80.

8. George E. Duckworth, *The Nature of Roman Comedy* (Princeton, 1952), pp. 244–245.

9. Durant, p. 69.

10. Duckworth, pp. 264–265.

11. Durant, pp. 65–66.

12. Ibid., pp. 75–77.

13. Northrop Frye, "The Argument of Comedy," *English Institute Essays (1948)*, ed. D. A. Robertson, Jr. (New York, 1949), pp. 58–73.

14. See Price, p. 41 ff.

15. Ibid., p. 52.

16. George H. Nettleton, "Sheridan's Introduction to the American Stage," *PMLA* 61 (1950): 165, 172 ff.

17. *The Rivals* programme folder, Theater Collection, New York Public Library at Lincoln Center, New York.
18. *The Autobiography of Joseph Jefferson* (New York, 1897), pp. 399–402.
19. Aug. 30, 1938.
20. *The Theatre World* 42, No. 254 (March, 1946): 20–21; 41, No. 250 (Nov., 1945): 5.
21. Ronald Bryden, *The Observer*, Oct. 9, 1966.
22. *Stage* (London), July 23, 1964.
23. Collie Knox, "Letter from London," *Morning Telegram*, May 17, 1971.
24. Unidentified review dated Feb. 6, 1925, in *The Rivals* clipping folder, Theater Collection, New York Public Library at Lincoln Center, New York.
25. Ibid.
26. *New York Times*, Jan. 15, 1942.

## St. Patrick's Day

1. Leo Hughes and A. H. Scouten, *Ten English Farces* (Austin, Texas, 1948), pp. 219–223.
2. Cecil Price, *The Dramatic Works of Richard Brinsley Sheridan*, Vol. I (Oxford, 1973), pp. 151–153.
3. *St. Patrick's Day* programme folder, Theater Collection, New York Public Library at Lincoln Center, New York.

## The Duenna

1. See above, pp. 10–11.
2. Cecil Price, *The Dramatic Works of Richard Brinsley Sheridan*, Vol. I (Oxford, 1973), p. 198 ff; Jack D. Durant, *Richard Brinsley Sheridan* (Boston, 1975), p. 85. Molière, Goldoni, and Dryden are often mentioned as other possible sources.
3. Price, pp. 199–209; Roger Fiske, "A Score for 'The Duenna,'" *Music and Letters* 42 (1961): 132–41.
4. Hyman Michelson, *The Jew in Early English Literature* (New York, 1926), p. 102; Edgar Rosenberg, "The Jew in Western Drama: An Essay" (1968), p. 24, in Edward D. Coleman, *The Jew in English Drama: An Annotated Bibliography* (New York, 1968).

5. Durant, p. 68.

6. Price, pp. 4, 215.

7. George H. Nettleton, "Sheridan's Introduction to the American Stage," *PMLA* 61 (1950): 165, 177–179.

8. *Lectures on the English Comic Writers* (1819), quoted in Price, p. 214.

9. R. D. Nussbaum, "Poetry and Music in 'The Duenna,' " *Westerly* 2 (1963): 58.

10. Victor Seroff, *Sergei Prokofiev: A Soviet Tragedy* (New York, 1968), p. 240.

11. *The Times* (London), 1970.

12. Alan Blyth, ibid., March, 1976.

For tapes and detailed reports of this revival, I am indebted to Dr. K. Mitchells of London, England.

## THE SCHOOL FOR SCANDAL

1. Thomas Moore, *Memoirs of the Life of the Rt. Hon. Richard Brinsley Sheridan (1858),* (New York, 1968), Vol. I, p. 139; Ian Donaldson, "Drama from 1710 to 1780," in *History of Literature in the English Language: Dryden to Johnson,* ed. Roger Lonsdale (London, 1971), p. 206.

2. Madeleine Bingham, *Sheridan: The Track of a Comet* (New York, 1972), p. 157; Cecil Price, *The Dramatic Works of Richard Brinsley Sheridan,* Vol. I (Oxford, 1973), p. 287.

3. Leonard Leff, "The Disguise Motif in Sheridan's *The School for Scandal,*" *Educational Theatre Journal* 22 (1970): 354 ff.

4. See above, p. 16.

5. Price, pp. 304–05.

6. George E. Duckworth, *The Nature of Roman Comedy* (Princeton, 1952), p. 245.

7. R. Crompton Rhodes, *The Plays and Poems of Richard Brinsley Sheridan,* Vol. II (1929), p. 13.

8. Ibid., pp. 5–6.

9. Quoted in Price, pp. 314–15.

10. J. R. De J. Jackson, "The Importance of Witty Dialogue in *The School for Scandal,*" *MLN* 76 (1961): 604.

11. Allan Rodway, "Goldsmith and Sheridan: Satirists of

Sentiment," in *Renaissance and Modern Essays Presented to Vivian de Sola Pinto*, ed. George R. Hibbard (New York, 1966), p. 68.

12. See Elizabeth M. Yearling, "The Good-Natured Heroes of Cumberland, Goldsmith, Sheridan," *Modern Language Review* 67 (1972): 490–500.

13. *The London Stage, 1660–1800*, Part 5: 1776–1800, ed. Charles Beecher Hogan (Carbondale, Illinois, 1968), p. clxxi.

14. Christian Deelman, "The Original Cast of *The School for Scandal*," *Review of English Studies* 13 (1962): 257–66.

15. Ibid., pp. 255–56.

16. George H. Nettleton, "Sheridan's Introduction to the American Stage," *PMLA* 65 (1950): 165, 172, 176–79.

17. Ernst Stahl, *Das englische Theater im 19. Jahrhundert* (Munich, Berlin, 1914), p. 228.

18. Program in *The School for Scandal* programme folder, Theater Collection, New York Public Library at Lincoln Center, New York.

19. *Daily Telegraph*, Ap. 6, 1874, quoted in Charles Eyre Pascoe, *The Dramatic List: A Record of the Principal Performances of Living Actors and Actresses on the British Stage* (London, 1879), p. 17.

20. Charles Morgan, *New York Times*, Dec. 15, 1929, X, 4.

21. *The Times* (London), March 28, 1933, p. 12.

22. Ibid., Jan. 21, 1949, p. 7; *Billboard*, March 19, 1949.

23. Caryl Brahms, *Plays and Players* 9 (May, 1962): 15; see also *New York Times*, Ap. 6, 1962, p. 31.

24. *The Times* (London), Jan. 21, 1949, p. 7.

25. *International Herald Tribune*, May 20–21, 1972, p. 8.

26. Helen Dawson, *The Observer* (London), May 14, 1972; see also ibid., Oct. 13, 1968, and *The Times* (London), Oct. 3, 1968, for reviews of the Nottingham production.

27. *New York Times*, June 5, 1923, p. 24.

28. Ibid., June 24, 1953, p. 29.

29. Ibid., Jan. 26, 1963.

30. Ibid., Nov. 22, 1966, p. 33.

## THE CRITIC

1. Jack D. Durant, *Richard Brinsley Sheridan* (Boston, 1975), pp. 108–09.

2. R. Crompton Rhodes, *The Plays and Poems of Richard Brinsley Sheridan*, Vol. II (New York, 1929), pp. 180–183.

3. Ibid., pp. 252–253.

4. *Morning Chronicle*, Nov. 1, 1779, and Nov. 2, 1779, quoted in Cecil Price, *The Dramatic Works of Richard Brinsley Sheridan*, Vol. II (Oxford, 1973), pp. 479–80.

5. See above, p. 16.

6. Rhodes, p. 181.

7. *The London Stage, 1660–1800*, Part 5: 1776–1800, ed. Charles Beecher Hogan (Carbondale, Ill. 1968), p. clxxii.

8. *The Critic* programme folder, Theater Collection, New York Public Library at Lincoln Center, New York.

9. *New York Times*, May 21, 1946, p. 19.

10. Ibid.

11. Eric Shorter, *Daily Telegraph*, Feb. 10, 1966.

## CONCLUSION

1. Allan Rodway, *English Comedy: Its Role and Nature from Chaucer to the Present Day* (Berkeley and Los Angeles, 1975), pp. 175–176.

2. See above, p. 17.

3. Susanne K. Langer, "The Great Dramatic Forms: The Comic Rhythm," *Feeling and Form* (New York, 1953), pp. 326–350.

4. Quoted in Ricardo Quintana, *Oliver Goldsmith: A Georgian Study* (New York, 1967), p. 141.

5. Louis Kronenberger, *The Thread of Laughter* (New York, 1952), pp. 200–202.

6. Program for Boston Museum performances, 1884, in *The School for Scandal* programme folder, Theater Collection, New York Public Library at Lincoln Center, New York.

7. Henry James, *The Scenic Art: Notes on Acting and the Drama, 1872–1901* (New Brunswick, 1948), p. 15.

# BIBLIOGRAPHY

### MODERN COLLECTED EDITIONS

Friedman, Arthur, ed. *Collected Works of Oliver Goldsmith*. 5 vols. Oxford, 1966.

Price, Cecil, ed. *The Dramatic Works of Richard Brinsley Sheridan*. 2 vols. Oxford, 1973.

### WORKS ABOUT GOLDSMITH

Behringer, Clara Marie. "A Production Prompt Book for *She Stoops to Conquer*." Unpublished M. A. thesis, University of Michigan. Ann Arbor, 1944.

Eichenberger, Karl. *Oliver Goldsmith: Das Komische in den Werken Seiner Reifeperiode*. Bern, 1954.

Heilman, Robert. "The Sentimentalism of Goldsmith's *Good-Natured Man*." In *Studies for William A. Read*. Baton Rouge, 1940.

Hopkins, Robert H. *The True Genius of Oliver Goldsmith*. Baltimore, 1969.

Gassman, Byron. "French Sources of Goldsmith's *The Good-Natured Man*." *PQ* 39 (1960): 59–62.

Lytton Sells, A. *Oliver Goldsmith: His Life and Works*. London and New York, 1974.

Quintana, Ricardo. "Goldsmith's Achievement as Dramatist." *University of Toronto Quarterly* 34 (1965): 159–77.

———. *Oliver Goldsmith: A Georgian Study*. New York, 1967.

Wardle, Ralph M. *Oliver Goldsmith*. Lawrence, Kansas, 1957.

## Works about Sheridan

Bingham, Madeleine. *Sheridan: The Track of a Comet*. New York, 1972.

Deelman, Christian. "The Original Cast of *The School for Scandal*." *Review of English Studies* 13 (1962): 257–266.

Durant, Jack D. *Richard Brinsley Sheridan*. Boston, 1975.

Fiske, Roger. "A Score for 'The Duenna'." *Music and Letters* 42 (1961): 132–41.

Jackson, J. R. De J. "The Importance of Witty Dialogue in *The School for Scandal*." *MLN* 76 (1961): 601–07.

Leff, Leonard. "The Disguise Motif in Sheridan's *The School for Scandal*." *Educational Theatre Journal* 22 (1970): 350–60.

Loftis, John Clyde. *Sheridan and the Drama of Georgian England*. Cambridge, Mass., 1977.

Moore, Thomas. *Memoirs of the Life of the Rt. Hon. Richard Brinsley Sheridan (1858)*. New York, 1968.

Nettleton, George H. "Sheridan's Introduction to the American Stage." *PMLA* 65 (1950): 163–82.

Nussbaum, R. D. "Poetry and Music in 'The Duenna'." *Westerly* 2 (1963): 58–63.

Rhodes, R. Crompton, ed. *The Plays and Poems of Richard Brinsley Sheridan*. 2 vols. New York, 1929.

Schiller, Andrew. "*The School for Scandal*: The Restoration Unrestored." *PMLA* 62 (1956): 694–704.

Sprague, Arthur. "In Defense of a Masterpiece: *The School for Scandal* Reexamined." *English Studies Today*. 3rd ser. Edinburgh, 1964.

## WORKS ABOUT COMEDY AND THE
## EIGHTEENTH-CENTURY THEATER

Appleton, William W. "The Double Gallant in Eighteenth Century English Comedy." In *English Writers of the Eighteenth Century*. Ed. John Middendorf. New York, 1971.

Crane, R. S. "Suggestions Toward a Genealogy of the 'Man of Feeling'." *ELH* 1 (1935): 205–230.

Duckworth, George E. *The Nature of Roman Comedy*. Princeton, 1952.

Frye, Northrop. "The Argument of Comedy." In *English Institute Essays (1948)*. Ed. D. A. Robertson, Jr. New York, 1949.

Hughes, Leo. *The Drama's Patrons: A Study of the Eighteenth-Century London Audience*. Austin, Texas, 1971.

Hughes, Leo, and A. H. Scouten. *Ten English Farces*. Austin, Texas, 1948.

Kronenberger, Louis. *The Thread of Laughter: Chapters on English Stage Comedy from Jonson to Maugham*. New York, 1952.

Langer, Suzanne K. "The Great Dramatic Forms: The Comic Rhythm." *Feeling and Form*. New York, 1953, pp. 326–350.

Leacroft, Richard. *The Development of the English Playhouse*. Ithaca, New York, 1973.

*The London Stage 1660–1800*. Part 5: 1776–1800. Ed. Charles Beecher Hogan. 3 vols. Carbondale, Ill., 1968.

Mander, Raymond, and Joe Mitchenson. *A Picture History of the British Theatre*. London, 1957.

Nicoll, Allardyce. *A History of English Drama: 1660–1900*. 5 vols. Cambridge, 1927.

Pascoe, Charles Eyre. *The Dramatic List: A Record of the Principal Performances of Living Actors and Actresses on the British Stage*. London, 1879.

Pedicord, Harry William. *The Theatrical Public in the Time of Garrick*. Carbondale, Ill., 1954.

Rodway, Allan. *English Comedy: Its Role and Nature*

*from Chaucer to the Present Day*. Berkeley, California, 1975.

————. "Goldsmith and Sheridan: Satirists of Sentiment." In *Renaissance and Modern Essays Presented to Vivian de Sola Pinto*. Ed. George R. Hibbard. New York, 1966.

Rosenfeld, Sybil. *A Short History of Scene Design in Great Britain*. Oxford, 1973.

Sherbo, Arthur. *English Sentimental Drama*. East Lansing, Mich., 1957.

Wimsatt, William K., Jr. *The Idea of Comedy*. Englewood, N.J., 1969.

Yearling, Elizabeth M. "The Good-Natured Heroes of Cumberland, Goldsmith, Sheridan." *Modern Language Review* 67 (1972): 490–500.

# INDEX